Red Giraffe

How to scale new heights and reach your goals

Hunter Leonard

Red Giraffe - How to scale new heights and reach your goals
Author: Hunter Leonard
Editor: Nicole Leonard
Cover Design & Layouts: Joanna Hassam
Publisher: Blue Frog Marketing Pty Ltd
website: www.bluefrogmarketing.com.au
First published in 2023 by Blue Frog Marketing Pty Ltd

National Library of Australia Cataloguing-in-Publication entry:
Author: Leonard, Hunter.

Title: Red Giraffe
Author: Hunter Leonard
Edition: 1st ed.
ISBN: Paperback -978-0-6452858-0-2 E-Book - 978-0-6452858-1-9
Bibliography.
Subjects: Small business-Small Business, Strategy
Dewey Number: 658.8

GOAL
MILESTONE
RESTPOINT
NO
THRU
ROAD
MILESTONE
THE BRIGHT
SHINY OBJECTS TREE
(AVOID - POISONOUS)
NO
THRU
ROAD
RIVER
CROSSING
DANGER!
START
RESTPOINT

CONTENTS

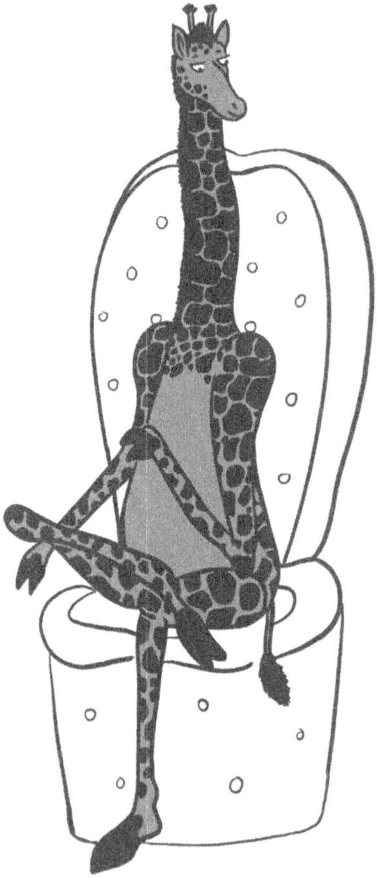

PRAISE FOR RED G

"Red G is a bright young giraffe. We are very proud of him"

Mama G and Dadda G

"Red G was one of those youngsters who you knew were bound for success. He is a hero with all the student G's"

Big G,
Red G's high school teacher.

"Red G is the coolest giraffe on the plains. We've all agreed to not eat him for lunch as it would seem to be a bit of a waste"

Lincoln the Lion
on behalf of the African
Savannah Predators Union
or ASPU.

"I've seen Red G, but never spoken to him face to face, for obvious reasons"

Mary the Meerkat

"He's just so damned smart and boy is he tall"

Anonymous.

PRAISE FOR HUNTER LEONARD

"Hunter is a true marketing professional. Hunter has broad ranging skill sets and knowledge which can greatly assist an organisations marketing needs. He scopes marketing problems in detail and takes time to think deeply about strategic marketing options. Hunter's style engenders trust and he is great to work with."

Michael Dawson
General Manager,
Marketing Bluescope Steel

"When at Australian Vinyls I engaged BlueFrog Marketing to conduct a survey of our major customers. Hunter was able to explore and identify the key issues that should be canvassed, and produce valuable insights in his analysis of the results. In addition the process was conducted so professionally that it increased our standing with the customers. Hunter is a pleasure to work with and I look forward to engaging him again."

Andrew Tulloch
National Sales & Marketing Manager
Australian Vinyls Corporation
A West Farmers Company

"Hunter is a consummate professional who is highly adaptable to various market sectors, he intently listens to your desired marketing outcomes and then delivers. It has been a pleasure knowing Hunter and his refreshing outlook that also entwines a community and social spirit."

Damian Seabrook
Altus Traffic

I started my first business aged 43. There were no 'how to run a business' blueprints to follow, so I made mistake after mistake.

Every time I made another expensive mistake, I had to search around for information on how to fix the mistake and make sure it didn't happen again. That meant that it took much longer (and caused many more sleepless nights) to turn a profit.

Eventually I made the business into a profitable commodity that someone wanted to buy, but it would have been so much quicker, easier and less stressful to have followed expert guidance.

When we go into business, generally we are good at the job (we're great 'technicians'), but we don't know how to run a business. My advice? Don't take the hard way like I did, learn the fast and easy way through Hunter.

Jan Reeves
SME Cash Collection Coach

I came across Hunter for the first time when I happened to reply to one of his posts on Linked In. This led to a meeting where we discussed business strategy and the market postioning of Investors Direct.

Hunter did a very thorough job in sourcing critical data and thus information of how we should shape our proposition and move toward a niche offer in a large market.

He interpreted my vision well and was able to capture it within a strategic marketing plan which straightened our focus and effort.

Client - Financial Services Industry

BlueFrog Marketing itself is a highly successful Marketing Consultancy and this is, without doubt, due to Hunter's vision, strategic mind, dedication to working for small-medium business and good old fashioned hard work. Hunter makes quality marketing accessible for organisations who thought it was beyond their reach.

Russell Powter
Experienced Advisor and Consultant

FOREWORD

Hunter and I have worked together across various organisations and projects for close to 25 years. Together, we have created a number of highly successful results for our business, and the communities in which we operate.

He is a trusted friend to our business, and I know he always seeks to have the best interests of our people and our business in mind.

Hunter is a tremendous listener who creates an environment where people can share their goals and vulnerabilities and as a result he builds strong relationships with people. He also subtly influences and has shown me that being different and being happy is ok in business and they are critical to making life work.

Hunter has a breadth of abilities that are much sought after, but seldom found, he can jump from strategy to compliance and capability to execution.

My view is that strategy is driven by whether or not change is required. Whether that is positive, negative or simply needed. I start with defining the desired state or outcome required and also spend time understanding why I need to change. I then go about understanding the steps backwards from the outcome required and attempt to define gaps in my current business value proposition.By thinking about your strategy in this way, your objectives are easily understood and hopefully, that garners support and create momentum.

It becomes real and quantifiable, provides logical connections to the desired outcome and most importantly gives you the energy you need to change your business.

"In short, the way I think about strategy is to think about the end state, reflect on what is required, identify gaps and then plug those gaps with what's required."

Once you've established a need, you must come back to the present and honestly assess where you are at, before you can then put your attention to working out what stepping stones you'll need to put in place to cross the river from where you are, to where you want to be.

Good intentions are great, but setting and achieving goals is really a behaviour. If you have some burning need or burning desire, you can put in place a strategy to get where you want to go. But then you actually have to do the work, consistently taking those steps, and keeping an eye on your progress with measurement.

Stick to your plan, because sometimes success can be just around the corner or just after the hardest part of the journey. There is nothing wrong with failing, but there is something wrong with not trying, and not working hard towards something that is important to you.

There is no doubt Hunter has contributed to my success, and I know I've also contributed to his. I am also certain if you apply the tips and advice in this book, you will be able to set and get your goals more often.

Lige Donald.
Steel Industry Executive

PREFACE

Would you like to become better at setting and achieving your goals?

This book is about strategy and strategic planning. Which in my opinion is the only proven method for doing just that.

I think Max McKeown says it all when he defined strategy as:

'the human attempt to get desirable ends with available means'

I'm a business owner, author and advcoate for mature age and I spend my life helping my clients research and plan their business and marketing strategy.

I work with a lot of individuals and organisations on setting and achieving goals.

I love what I do.

But for whatever reason, many business owners don't fall in 'love' with the idea of strategy. They're happy to set goals, but they find the idea of strategy and planning confusing and unapproachable.

My purpose in writing this book is to make strategy more accessible to the average person and the average business owner.

It doesn't have to be complicated, so let us simplify it.

There are a lot of books about strategy and I agree that some of them are difficult to understand making them difficult to apply. Even for someone who knows a thing or two about strategy and who has spent the best part of thirty-five years writing strategic plans.

We set goals and we achieve them. Over the past twenty years, we've helped more than 500 clients achieve revenue growth of over $2 billion dollars doing just this.

Of course, we've helped them achieve many more goals as well. Goals such as higher satisfaction scores from clients, greater connection to the communities they operate in, more productive marketing results and a lot more

The missing point in most of these books is the purpose of strategy.

Why do it at all?

PREFACE

Put simply, strategy is just a tool (or a set of tools) to help you reach your dreams and goals.

Without these tools, a goal can diminish to a wish. Something you hope for, but can never quite achieve. Or something you are working towards, but you don't know how you are progressing and where you don't know how far you've come.

Strategy is exactly like a long walk in the bush - something I love to do. A journey to a destination you love, or have been thinking about. It is the way you manage each and every step, it is what you put in your back pack, it is the milestones along the way.

When you keep it simple, strategy ceases to be confusing and becomes easy and perhaps even a joy to use.

I hope you enjoy the journey through this book, and that by the end, you will be more comfortable using strategy to achieve the things that matter most to you.

A thriving business, a home for your family, a comfortable retirement, a big impact on a social problem that you are concerned about. Whatever your goals, this book will give you the tools and tips to achieve them.

Good luck.

CHAPTER ONE
THE STORY OF THE RED GIRAFFE

CHAPTER ONE - THE STORY OF THE RED GIRAFFE

I'm a scientist by training - having studied botany and land management at Macquarie University.

Whilst I'm not a biologist I am fascinated by the great diversity of animals and insects we have on this planet.

There are a number of evolutionary ideas about why giraffes got long necks. The one we've chosen to use is that they were naturally selected over hundreds of thousands of years as slightly longer and longer necks gave access to food that other species could not get to on the grasslands and open woodlands in Africa.

In other words, constant stretching and effort to reach a goal (food) selected out those with longer necks for survival who then passed on their genes for longer necks to their offspring.

There are a number of reasons why we chose to use a giraffe as the icon for my latest book.

The first was because my wife and business partner - Nicole - loves the name.

The second is we kind of like coloured animals around here - after all one of our businesses is called Blue Frog Marketing, and we have an owl as the icon for another business - Silver & Wise.

Most importantly the giraffe is a great visual representation of reaching high for your goals. And no one is better in the animal world at setting their sights high and reaching for the stars than Red G. He is an inspiration.

This is not a debate about why giraffes got their long necks, it is about using that as an analogy for setting star high goals and stretching yourself and/or your business to achieve them.

CHAPTER TWO
FIGHTING FIRES AND MANAGING TIME

Red-G's Guide to Managing Time

Make time for the important stuff

Use tools that help you work out what the important stuff is

Stop doing the unimportant stuff

Keep filling your day with the important stuff

Remember to not do the unimportant stuff when you find yourself slipping

CHAPTER TWO - FIGHTING FIRES AND MANAGING TIME

There is a crucial factor in strategy and strategic planning whose importance cannot be overestimated.

That is your willingness to invest the time and energy required to be more strategic in your approach to running your business.

There is no magic in this book that will - without effort - materialise wealth and riches for you.

This book is about the steady, planned road to success, not the instant riches or fame approach.

So if you are after instant riches and fame, without effort, then stop reading right now, and see if you can return this book to the place of purchase or to the author.

I can't really do anything about your willingness - that has to come from you.

I can promise that if you apply yourself, put aside the time to use these tools honestly and well. Learn them so they become second nature to you. Then you will be able to expand and grow whatever enterprise you are trying to run.

That enterprise could be a personal development project, it could be a community-based organisation or it could be a for-profit business.

I don't want you to consider me a guru, or the source of your success.

I just want to share these tools - some of my own creation, and many from other smart people around the world.

These tools are only as good as your willingness to use them. Beyond your willingness, there is also a little thing called Time.

Time seems to be the arch-enemy of all of us. Especially in business.

There never seems to be enough time to get things done. Many, if not most business owners would say that time is one of their biggest challenges.

It is why I am covering off the issue of time management before we even get to discussing strategy and the tools of strategic planning.

The solution is making time to make time. I know that sounds odd, but simply put unless you can create some time to do these things, you'll never get out of the cycle of not having enough time.

So what are the real barriers to not having enough time?

In my experience in the two decades of running my own business and also consulting to more than 500 other businesses, I have concluded there are six reasons why we don't have enough time.

They are:

1. We don't plan
2. We don't organise ourselves with good systems and processes for getting things done
3. We don't properly learn how to do things, or try to do things best left to experts
4. We allow others to control our schedule
5. We don't learn from mistakes by putting in solutions, and so we keep making the same mistakes over and over
6. We don't schedule the more important things in our day first, letting unimportant things rule the clock

Each of these has a solution of course. Some can be instituted immediately, some may take some time to put in place.

But recognising each of these six areas in your own life is a great start to acting on them.

Here is an action plan and benchmark you can use to take control to your schedule and make time to make time:

1. Schedule a time in your diary now to read this book, and once read to spend time each day/week to work on your business strategy. Do not let this time be overrun with anything else - ever. Unless there is a fire or a major illness in the family.

2. Look over your business and see what systems and processes you have in place for strategic planning, money management, marketing, selling, quality, people and so forth. Where there is a lack of systems, or the systems are not working for you, make a note and begin putting in place those systems.

3. Look over your business and decide on those things that you find difficult or that consume a lot of time for you. Make a plan to increase your skills in these areas or hire an expert to do them for you. For instance if you find book keeping a real challenge, then get a book keeper to do it.

4. Put in place a policy from today onwards that you control your own diary - put times in your diary yourself or assign someone in your team to control it for you. Do not let others control these things. If you've decided you are doing strategic planning at 11am on Monday, then make sure you are UNAVAILABLE at that time for anything else.

5. If there has been a recent mistake, look at what you did to rectify if, and see if there is now a program or system in place to avoid that mistake in the future. An example might be, an invoice wasn't sent to a client, or work was done before the invoice was paid when you have a policy that no work is to be done before payment. Reinforce or write the policy and ensure all your team know it. Retrain or correct the person who did the work before payment so they don't do it again.

6. At the start of each week, or indeed as a standard schedule put in place times to do key things each week. For instance a staff meeting, or strategic planning, or a time to do invoices, or a time to call potential clients or current customers. Keep these times sacrosanct(which means regarding a routine or something else as too important or valuable to be interfered with)

In terms of time management tools, there are some awesome resources available to you as well. Below I've included an essay on Time Management that I wrote for our business ownership course and a module on time management.

TIME MANAGEMENT MODULE - BUSINESS OWNERS COURSE

In the recent client roadshow, I presented an introduction to marketing entitled “Get your Marketing Cooking”.

As part of that presentation, I decided to help all attendees get a start on their marketing plan by doing a short SWOT Analysis Exercise.

After that exercise, I individually reviewed the notes they handed in and sent a personal email to each attendee around the country – over 120 in total.

Out of those 120 responses, 118 principals said that their greatest weakness and challenge was time management. I understand that not all pressures on your time are things that you can control.

And yet, the simple tools presented in this essay will go a long way to helping you be in more control of your time than ever before.

Some very effective individuals in history including well-known authors and military leaders have developed these tools – one was even developed by a former president of the USA – Eisenhower.

Like all our modules, we are acting as a curator and guide for best business practice and we commend these tools to you.

Like any of the other modules in our business ownership program, the tools themselves do nothing. It is your learning and daily application of these tools that will get the results.

TIME, TIME - IF ONLY I HAD MORE TIME.

Time demands are amongst the most common sources of pressure, stress and tension in our personal and business lives.

Unfortunately, for business owners and high performing individuals it seems the more you strive for, and the more you achieve the higher the demands on your time.

I have a colleague who says "If you want something done, give it to a busy person" and I can see the logic in this statement. People who are active and busy always seem to get lots done.

But this does not mean you can't be efficient and effective in how you use your time.

As a business owner, you will find that as you grow your business and bring on staff, and get more customers – the types of work you need to be doing will change. You hand over tasks to staff and so forth.

However, only those business owners who work out for themselves the difference between 'busy work' and 'effective work' will ever be successful in building strong, prosperous organisations. They also have to be responsible for having every staff member practicing the same principles of effective time management in their roles too.

Time is precious, and you have to spend it on the things that make a difference, not just on things that have to be done.

No one can decide for you what is urgent and important in your life. Urgent being something that has to be done now. Important being something that contributes to long-term life or business goals. Imagine not doing something and consider if it would place your long-term goals at risk. If the answer is YES it is important to you. If no, it falls into another box.

THE EISENHOWER PRINCIPLE

President Dwight Eisenhower was quoted as saying "I have two kinds of problems: the urgent and the important. The urgent are not important, and the important are never urgent." He used a matrix – now called the Eisenhower Matrix to structure how he prioritized his work. In my favourite US political drama – The West Wing – there is a quote from Leo McGarry – the President's Chief of Staff – he said "we're trying to keep the knucklehead stuff of the President's Desk today" I love that – your goal is to keep the 'knucklehead' stuff off your own desk using this tool - see image on the next page.

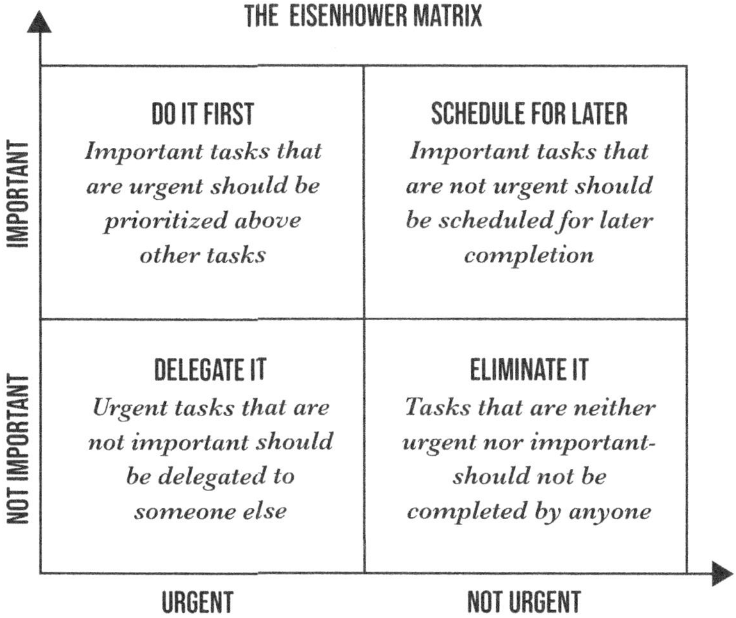

In the DO box are things, which are urgent and important. You do these now.

In the DECIDE box are important things which are not urgent – you schedule a time to do these.

The DELEGATE box contains things, which are urgent but not important, and you should be finding someone who can do these for you.

The last box contains not urgent, not important things and as it says here you should DELETE these from your routine. When you are procrastinating about something, these are often things you will find yourself doing, but which add no value to your business or to your family or life.

DO IT, DELEGATE IT, DUMP IT

This three-category system is another time management tool you can use. You simply write your battle plan or to do list, and then categorise everything on it into the three boxes.

From there it is very simple – Do the things only you can do that are important. Delegate the things that someone else can do for you, Dump those things that don't matter at all.

You may think as a sole trader that there is no one else to do the second category for you, and you can't afford staff to do them.

But in today's service economy there are numerous alternatives to full time employees such as:

UPWORK – an online portal where you can load projects and get people from around the world to quote on completing them for you. I recently outsourced a design job for my latest book and got over 100 illustrations drawn for under $500. There are lots of these portals available now including FIVERR and others.

OUTSOURCING – you can hire a full-time employee in the Philippines for around a third of the cost of a local employee. If you don't want to hire overseas and can't afford a full-time employee, then get someone to do it part-time, or find a student, or outsource it to a company that provides these admin services.

BIG ROCKS

The Big Rocks analogy is often credited to Stephen Covey, but he himself was referencing a professor he once heard use this analogy. A little more philosophical in its approach than others we've mentioned previously – the BIG ROCKS analogy is as follows.

The professor says to his class he is going to fill a jar – and shows a range of items on his desk including some rocks, pebbles, sand and water.

He puts the big rocks into the jar and fills it up to the rim and then holds it up and asks the students if it is full. They all nod in agreement.

He then adds the small pebbles, which fill up cracks between the big rocks and repeats the question – once again they all nod.

By the addition of the sand, they've all got wise. Of course he pours in the sand and it fills the spaces between the pebbles.

Lastly he adds the water, which then fills up all the remaining space, and the jar is truly full.

The point of the analogy is that you have to put the big rocks in first. The Big Rocks being representative of the important stuff in your life.

Unfortunately a lot of us fill our LIFE JAR with unimportant water and sand. And if they are put in first there is no room for the BIG ROCKS,

Whilst we may not have time to do things, we should never get into the situation where we fail to do the BIG ROCK things because other stuff is in the way. And yet as business owners we fail to do strategic planning, we fail to talk to customers, we fail to manage our cashflow – surely all BIG ROCK things in relation to business – using the excuse that we are just too busy doing paperwork, or admin or, or, or..

WHAT HAVEN'T YOU FINISHED?

Do me a favour and have a look at your in-tray or email inbox. If you're not near the in-tray whilst you are reading this, then visualise it in your mind.

Is it empty? Is it overflowing? Is there anything in your in-tray or inbox that you might have picked up a few times or looked at several times, only to not handle it because you can't do it right now, or because you got interrupted?

You might be surprised to learn that one of the most compelling and time wasting thing in our lives is the number of incomplete tasks and projects we have.

The only way to solve this is to do an efficiency exercise called the FINISHING GAME. We ran a workshop on this process with my team a few years back, and the impact it had on their productivity was amazing.

All of them had in-trays with things they hadn't finished and so we blocked out a full half-day, turned the phones to message bank, and made them clean out their in-tray with the following rules:

They could only handle a piece of paper or email once. As soon as they picked it up, they had to finish it. If it meant calling a supplier, or filing the document, or paying the bill – whatever it was, it HAD to be done there and then.

If the action was to ask a question of someone else, or hand the item to the next person that was allowed, but then the next person in the 'line' had to then action their steps right away too.

By the end of the session, they had empty in-trays, and organised and filed papers, documents and emails.

It was incredible how quickly it was all done, and interestingly how much work they all got done in the next week or so because they had nothing that was drawing their attention away that hadn't been completed.

I always follow this methodology with my work, and from then on we scheduled monthly 'catch up' sessions – which eventually only had to go for 30 mins because everyone was keeping their in-trays up to date and their inboxes under control.

In fact, the writing of this module is being done because it was a backlog from earlier this week, and I got interrupted – so I'm catching up now. As it turns out I was waiting for a piece of information from another individual, so I just got on the phone and called them, got the information and then started on the writing of this unit.

TEN SIMPLE TIPS ON TIME MANAGEMENT

Use a calendar – if you find yourself not getting to certain tasks – like doing the books, or meeting your team for a review – then schedule it in the diary just like any other appointment – and make it a 'crime' to cancel any of these appointments. It's amazing if you force yourself to set and keep appointments to do stuff, how it actually gets done.

Put a time limit on a task – you'd be surprised how much you will get done if you limit the time to get it done

Set reminders for scheduled tasks – if you don't remind yourself you'll find the time scheduled for 'doing the books' or other things will be lot because you forgot or got distracted

Distraction free zone – if you have to turn off your phone for an hour, or turn off email notifications then DO IT. Remove the things that distract you and focus on the task at hand. If you find yourself jumping from one thing to another STOP IT, and focus

Use the tools we've provide to prioritise – don't complain about not getting to important stuff – turn it around

Learn to say NO – particularly to things that don't add value. I don't take meetings from unsolicited media calls anymore.

Battle Plan – I'm 10x more effective if I list out what I have to do each day – use a piece of paper or an APP like Monday or Trello and organise yourself.

Do similar things together – if you have a range of financial tasks, do these all together whilst you're on a roll. Don't jump from sales to finance to admin to marketing.

Delegate – use others to do the KNUCKLEHEAD stuff. You may actually be really inefficient at filing or marketing – why not get an expert to do it if it's not a good use of your time

DO IT – don't just learn about time management – put it into practice – use the Eisenhower Matrix, Big Rocks, Battle Plans – whatever works for you. Stop complaining about it, and take control

I'd also like to recommend a book to you. Written by a friend in our DENT Global Entrepreneurs program - *SMART Time Investment for Business by Kate Christie* provides 128 tips for managing time better.

It is an excellent read and goes into the subject of Time Management in a lot more detail than I have here.

CHAPTER THREE
A WORD ON THE IMPORTANCE OF STRATEGY

Red-G on Strategy

Every goal I've ever set myself, I achieved through strategy.

Set yourself a goal

Think about the action that will help you get to that goal

Do those actions

Stay on the path

Reach your goal

Celebrate reaching your goal

Set a new goal

CHAPTER THREE - A WORD ON THE IMPORTANCE OF STRATEGY

Goals, purpose, culture, strategy, planning, execution, money, people.

Which of these things is more important?

Supposedly Peter Drucker said 'culture eats strategy for breakfast'. It is a well known theme and the subject of many a 'meme'.

But it ain't true. Not only that he said it, which he didn't.

But even if he had, it wouldn't be true anyway.

Yes, this is my opinion, but it is one based on observation and experience.

CHAPTER THREE - A WORD ON THE IMPORTANCE OF STRATEGY

If you look at this universe we live in, and observe life around you, and think about your own life and things you have done, you already intuitively know that where we are headed, or what we are trying to do is the most important thing.

Plants do it when they grow towards the sun.

Salmon do it when they swim upstream.

Everyone does it, everyday of our lives.

We set out to do something, go somewhere and then we do it.

This is all very well for a simple task of walking to the end of the street, or getting dressed, or finding some food to eat.

But what about longer, more complex goals, where it isn't clear the exact sequence of steps we need to take to reach it.

What about handling the barriers and diversions that we encounter along the way? What about the direct opposition or the competition from others trying to reach the same goal.

That is where strategy comes in - the smart ideas, plans and actions that someone puts in place to reach a stated goal.

That is where passion comes in - the desire to get to that goal above all else.

That is where persistence comes in - the willingness to run into challenges, and despite everything in your way, still aim to reach that goal.

In my business life, I've come across a lot of business owners and people who wish for something, but don't want to or can't do the work needed to turn that wish into a goal that can be achieved.

They don't want to, or don't have the skills to think strategically.

They don't have the willingness or the persistence to put in the daily, weekly or monthly effort it will take to keep persisting towards that goal.

They get sidetracked, they want the magic bullet without the work.

The passive income stream with no effort.

I wrote this book to show that star high goals can be set, and they can be achieved. And there are many, many tools you can use to achieve these things. I wrote it to inspire those who are willing to work for their goals, for the things they are passionate about. Good luck on your journey to your star high goal.

Throughout this book, I'm going to be sharing a lot of ideas, tools and processes that I use everyday myself. They are not theoretical, they are practical tools - just like a hammer or a shovel.

They are not all tools of my own creation. I have studied and read hundreds of books and courses from some of the world's best strategic thinkers.

I'll share where I got these tools from and the inventor of them when I reference them.

I consider myself a generalist and some time ago came up with this quote as a way of describing my role in business - "the role of a generalist is to foster communication amongst specialists"

As an author, I have a passion to share successful actions and ideas. To bring together disparate source of information into a useful toolkit for my readers.

I don't need to be, nor care to be known as, the source of every good idea ever invented. I don't want to be seen as a guru.

I just want to help, and the main purpose of this book - like all my others - is to help you.

CHAPTER FOUR
THE 7 STRATEGIC HABITS OF SUCCESSFUL COMPANIES

Red G's Habits

Always look for the tallest tree

Stretch way up and eat
whatever food you find up there

Remember where the best
trees are

Make sure you share with others

Never eat more than you can run
off in a single chase with a lion

Acting hungry is good, being
hungry is bad

CHAPTER FOUR - THE 7 STRATEGIC HABITS OF SUCCESSFUL COMPANIES

Some time ago, I published an article talking more about the values related to strategy, as opposed to strategic planning itself.

These values are in some respects superior in importance that the strategy itself.

Why?

Because, knowing them, you can come up with your own methods and approach to meeting or keeping these values in for your organisation.

For example, one value is around being connected to the customer.

You could read this, and say well surveys are fine, but I really want to have any advisory board made up of key customers who can work with me to ensure we service all customers really well. And I would say - awesome idea - that would work really well.

You've created a great strategic tool or idea out of understanding what values you need to have in your business to be successful.

Here is that article, reprinted in full.

STRATEGY

The dictionary defines strategy as:

"a plan of action designed to achieve a long term or overall aim" "a method or plan chosen to bring about a desired future"

"the art and science of planning and marshalling resources for their efficient and effective use"

Some of the important themes here are:

- a plan
- action
- desired future/goals
- efficiency
- effectiveness
- making decisions

Let's discuss the importance of strategy to any business owner – it can also be referred to as working ON the business rather than IN the business.

CHAPTER FOUR - THE 7 STRATEGIC HABITS OF SUCCESSFUL COMPANIES

Have you ever seen a hurdler running a race – they don't just jump the hurdles – you'll see they have worked out how many steps they take in between hurdles and in a sense they are preparing for each jump two or three steps before each hurdle.

Many business owners wear a blindfold, run into the hurdle, fall over and then get up and run in the wrong direction – all because they didn't have a plan, and no strategy to prepare for the hurdles ahead.

When we discuss tools later in this book like the SWOT Analyses, or PESTLE or Porters 5-forces – these are all tools that have been designed to help business owners assess their market, customers and them- selves in order to make decisions and get some visibility on the future so they can PLAN ahead.

For today's business owner – operating in competitive markets – it actually isn't acceptable to make excuses like:

- I don't understand strategy
- I don't have time
- I've got too much work to do today
- I'm busy with customers

Because if you want to achieve your desirable future – you need to have a strategy – decisions made, plans drawn up, hurdles identified – in order to get where you want to go.

This book is all about reinforcing this importance, and helping you learn some of the tools that are available to you to help the process such as:

- what you should have in a business plan
- the areas of your business you need to apply strategic planning and thinking toward
- what types of strategic tools are available to you

However, despite all that we discuss in this book – you also have at your disposal the most wonderful skills and tools ever invented which are:

- your ability to dream and set goals for yourself
- your ability to make a decision
- your willingness to have a go, take a risk
- your resilience to overcome tough times and barriers
- along the journey

Never forget these innate abilities and skills – back yourself and use them.

Now let's talk about the seven key habits of successful business owners in relation to strategy.

These habits will become your guidepost for developing and maintaining a strategic focus in your business. These habits along with the questions we list in the 'strategy review guide' form the basis of successful strategy in any business.

We have given these 7 habits an acronym – C.U.S.T.O.M.A.

This acronym will help you remember the 7 habits in the Model.

In simple terms, it stands for **C**ustomer, **U**nderstanding, **S**elective, **T**ruth, **O**penness, **M**easured and Adaptable)

You should always be asking questions in business. Never think you have the answer.

If you ever think you have the answer your 'spidey sense' should immediately go on alert – because this is when we are most vulnerable – when we assume we know what's going on or have all the answers.

HABIT 1 - THEY ARE ORGANISED AROUND THE CUSTOMER

Something that is very common about businesses that are stuck in a rut, or don't know what to do with their marketing to get growth is they are not organised around the customer.

But what does this mean?

Have you ever walked into a business in a retail environment and stood around waiting for ages to be served, even though there were lots of staff sitting at their desks within view of you, none of them looked up or acknowledged you – because it wasn't their job.

In fact sometimes it feels like they are actively avoiding you whilst they do something that is obviously highly important on their computer or desk.

You know the feeling.

Look at the organisation chart of most businesses and really they are organised around the leader of a business, or department on job functions or responsibilities.

The very look and feel of an organisation chart is one of fixed structure, stuck boxes, NO FLOW – other than up and down amongst the staff.

Consider a more circular model with the customer at the centre of the circle or at the pupil of your eye(for example).

In this way, all the activities of the business are visually and physically, and philosophically and actionably organised around the customer.

You've already experienced businesses like this.

Walking into Officeworks in the last few months has been a completely different experience than in the past. There is someone at the entry to greet you, almost every staff member you walk past looks you in the eye and says hello. They are obviously there to serve you, not pushy mind you, but definitely aware and respectful of your presence.

Same goes for the VIC ROADS office – My past experience was of a very bureaucratic organisation – you actually felt like you were in a govt department.

But the other day I walked in to register my new car, and there was a bright, bubbly and smiling concierge to greet me, ask me what I needed and to direct me to a very specific location in the office where I got rapid and friendly service.

Yes, I still got a number from a machine, there was still a short wait, but the greeting and the directing was a perfect way to acknowledge I was here, and I was going to be served professionally.

Ever experienced this? Ever experienced a restaurant where you just can't seem to catch the eye of the staff, and meanwhile they are all standing around the counter talking to each other and not looking at or being aware of the patrons at the tables?

How else can a business be organised around a customer? There are many ways, here's a list:

- They survey regularly
- They are super quick to answer phones, emails, complaints, enquiries
- They are friendly and professional
- They acknowledge quickly when they make a mistake and fix it for you, sometimes even going beyond just the fix to add value

- They add value in transactions
- They know their product and can help you
- They are observant, acknowledge your presence and other friendly human interactions
- Their process from your first enquiry to doing business to deliveries etc are all clear, friendly and professional
- Their products and services are exactly as promised
- They are human, they make mistakes, but they fix them.
- They don't offer bureaucracy or stops in the way of helping you – "oh that's not my job"
- Their offices and premises are clean, inviting and easy to navigate
- They are easy to do business with
- They know your needs and wants implicitly
- They know you

HABIT 2 – THEY HAVE A THIRST FOR UNDERSTANDING

In today's world, it seems many businesses are getting further and further away from their customers, and more an more insulated inside their business.

We've benchmarked more than 1200 business owners, and found that very few – less than 20% seem to be interested in what is going on with their customers in terms of needs and wants, or trends in their market place, or how competitors are changing their strategies or campaigns.

CHAPTER FOUR - THE 7 STRATEGIC HABITS OF SUCCESSFUL COMPANIES

Running a business is tough, and there are a lot of pressures on business owners and staff to get the 'day to day' done in their job. They feel like they don't have time to work on the business and whilst this may be a fact, it can also be used as an excuse.

The fact is, a business which is disconnected from it's market, customers, competitors or even it's own position in the market is far less likely to survive than a business with a thirst for understanding.

To do otherwise is really leaving future prosperity, success or even survival to chance. It is blaming conditions or the way it is for not being in touch with your surroundings – which equate to market, customers and competitors in a business sense.

Imagine trying to get up from your desk at the office and making it all the way home with a blindfold and a set of noise blocking headphones on. You might find it pretty hard, and in fact it might be incredibly dangerous.

Consider the equally dangerous situation of running a business with no awareness of what is going on.

Having a thirst for knowledge and understanding is a mission critical skill for any business owner. It keeps you on top of the trends, aware of customer needs, and conscious of what the competition are doing.

It isn't hard, and there are many simple tools for researching a market, surveying customers, and observing competitors.

But it isn't an option. And you can't make excuses. You simply must do it to survive and prosper.

HABIT 3 – THEY ARE SELECTIVE

Sometimes in today's economy it can feel very much like there is information overload for a business owner.

Content marketing is all the rage, and along with customer communications, financial communications, staff communications etc, it can all seem too much and cause a business owner to reject all the information or feel tired and irritable in having to handle another piece of data.

A great business owner is selective. They have in place policies and procedures to select the important from the unimportant in their business.

This isn't necessarily a skill that is native to a human being. We have five senses and they are turned on all the time. Sure we could shut our eyes, or we could put on headphones, or we could just zone it out. And sure some people are good at concentrating in noisy situations. And some do in fact wear headphones on their way to work or school to cut off some of these information flows.

However, the downside to this is an absence of important information. I'm sure you've seen someone with headphones on walk out in front of traffic, or walk into another person on the street because they weren't fully aware of their surroundings.

In business, you want to have full awareness of what is going on, but you also need the ability to select out the important stuff too. You want the best of both worlds.

Putting aside the innate ability to do this, there are in fact a lot of strategic business tools that can help you select the important from the unimportant and make decisions on that information.

Tools like the SWOT Analysis (strengths, weaknesses, opportunities and threats) and the PESTLE Analysis (Political, Economic, Social, Technology, Legal and Environmental trends) were designed for just that purpose.

Segmenting a market and selecting a target customer group is also a strategy designed to help a business focus.

Using tools like this will give a business owner what seems like a superhuman ability to run a focused and profitable business. Superhuman to those business owners who aren't aware these tools exist and live their lives running from one urgent task to another, never finding a priority focus to help them prosper in their business.

The great business owner is able to be SELECTIVE and as a result, enjoys an environment that is far more under their control than those who are dispersed and can't focus or don't have the tools to focus their energy.

HABIT 4 - THEY SEEK THE TRUTH

Many business owners are operating off assumptions about their customers, business and market that are out of date, incomplete or just plain WRONG.

You can hide behind assumptions all you like. You can hope for the best in a business, but the fact is, unless you know the TRUE VALUE of what you do in the context of customer needs and wants and in comparison to what else is available in a market you will not survive for long.

History is littered with examples of both market segments and individual businesses who held onto outdated assumptions, product offerings or solutions and were passed by due to changes in needs, behaviours, government or other factors.

We no longer ride horse and buggies because cars came along, but I'll guarantee you that somewhere on the planet at that time was a business who stubbornly clung to the hope that those damn infernal smoky automobiles would never last.

More recently, witness the desperate moves by taxis to block UBER drivers via legal action. Prior planning and preparation and understanding of customers may have reduced the impact of UBER.

Taxis' could have "UBERED" themselves before UBER even arrived.

If a business owner operates a business centred on the customer, has a thirst for knowledge and is able to select the important facts and information out of the data available to them in a market, they will be able to identify a TRULY VALUED POSITION for themselves in any marketplace. This doesn't mean they'll be able to execute it, and because they don't have the resources to change, they may still go out of business. But at least they will have done the best they can, and in most cases a strong strategic process will lead to a better chance of survival and prosperity.

What is TRUTH in terms of value?

They have tools, procedures and systems which support open communication – visible signage, working phone systems, emails that get answered, an interest in customer feed back, and a willingness to solve any issues that arise

HABIT 5 – THEY ARE OPENLY COMMUNICATING

A business that knows its own TRUTH is one thing. But many businesses don't do any where near enough to let their customers, prospects and market know what they have to offer.

In our benchmark, less than 20% of companies have a written marketing plan. Less than 15% have communicated to existing customers in the past 12 months, less than 5% are measuring what marketing works.

In short, companies underestimate and under-do what is required to grow their businesses profitably. Sure many are reasonably successful, they get referrals – but many are doing less than they could with a strong program of communication to the market, prospects and customers.

Many companies also lose a fair percentage of their customers each year – a phenomenon called CHURN RATE – meaning they have to find quite a few new clients just to retain their sales or profit from the year before.

A habit of openness – or if you like willingness to communicate A LOT about your company to your market, customers and prospects is a prerequisite to continued growth, profitability and survival.

Here are five elements, which demonstrate a business that is practicing openness:

1. They have a written marketing plan and regular communication going out to existing customers, new prospects and the wider market via PR, social media and news outlets

2. They have someone responsible for the marketing effort – this could be the business owner or a marketing assistant or an outsourced marketing person or agency.

3. They have clear positioning statements and communication messages which communicate their value to their customers

4. They deliver on their promises to customers in relation to this value – in other words received value (after purchase) is at least as good as perceived value(prior to purchase)

5. They are growing in relation to their market – markets grow fast or slow, but an open communicating business will usually be growing faster than the average in their market

HABIT 6 - THEY ARE ALWAYS MEASURED

In the old western movies, you sometimes saw a person lean down and put their ear to the train tracks or ground to listen and see if a train or horses were coming. The theory being you could hear the sound in the metal or ground before you could actually see the train or horses.

The saying 'keeping your ear to the ground' comes from this, and this habit is incredibly important in business. No I don't mean putting your ear on the ground in your office. I mean using some sort of method to listen to the market or your customers or some sort of measurement to find out what marketing is working.

A business that has its ear to the ground will be more successful than one who doesn't because simply put, they are more aware of the environment and also knowledgeable about successful and unsuccessful actions in their business.

There are many, many ways you can measure your marketing strategy.

In this article, I'm going to share 5 habits for successfully measuring the performance of your marketing.

IF YOU CAN'T MEASURE IT, DON'T DO IT

A well worn saying is 'I know 50% of my advertising is working, I just don't know which 50%' which is attributed to John Wanamaker who co-incidentally was the first person to ever use a price tag in his general store in the USA.

I personally would reject this situation, as I can't afford to waste half my investments in my business, and I'm sure you are the same.

This is why we advise clients to make sure they work out how they are going to measure a marketing program before they even commit to it. And if they can't work out a simple measure, then we say don't do it.

THE GOLDEN QUESTION

One of the simplest of marketing measures and one that is so so important is what we call the golden question. It is 'Where did you hear about us?'

In an instant, this gives you a guide as to what marketing has delivered that customer to you. And if asked over time to many customers, will give you a trend for the best channel to be promoting yourself. Now some 'experts' will say – but the customer won't remember, or maybe they saw a few different ads in different places before coming to you.

Frankly I don't care. Whatever ad or promotion is the one they remember I will increase my investment in, and if that was the one that brought them in, I'm happy with that as a measure. This question should be a critical 'must do' in any first contact discussion with a new customer.

MEASUREMENT BY OBSERVATION

You don't have to survey customers or prospects to get information about what people like and don't like. You can simply observe them in a shopping centre. We've conducted many observation studies in food courts, and shops simply observing how people move through a store or location, what they interact with, how they choose a store and so forth.

If you have a retail store, stand in the store and simply observe people, and you may find out some inter- esting information about where to place advertising, point of sale and which products to keep or discard.

There are many ways to build knowledge, information and measure.

ROI

A simple template we use is a RETURN ON INVESTMENT calculation. This adds up sales from a marketing program and divides this by costs to get a ratio. For example if you make 20% margin on revenue, you need a ratio of $5 for every $1 invested to break even.

We've changed marketing programs and compared alternative campaigns finding differences of up to 20 times on ROI for the same investment.

Using this comparison you can prioritise where to spend your marketing dollar.

WHAT MEASURES SUCCESS?

A good habit is working out what success looks like for a campaign before you start it.

For example a customer is worth $500 to you on average. Let's say you were looking at running a Google campaign for $5,000. We can simply say that we would need at least 10 customers for that campaign to break even.

If you look at that campaign and think it unlikely you will get 10 customers then you can make a decision on whether to do the campaign in the first place.

HABIT 7 - THEY ARE ADAPTABLE

This habit is so important, we've even given it its own module in our business ownership courses and coaching.

"It is not the strongest of the species that survives, nor the most intelligent that survives. It is the one that is most adaptable to change" Charles Darwin

I personally like this saying a lot. Strength and Intelligence are fine attributes to have in a business or marketing sense. However, as many business owners will know from experience, the only constant in business is CHANGE.

Unfortunately for many businesses, and categories in markets it seems like the game is to find a way to do something and then keep doing it as long as possible, resisting change until there is no other solution but to go out of business or jump on the new way to do it.

You can't blame businesses – often a lot of investment goes into infrastructure to manufacture products in a certain way, or a lot of investment goes into training staff to deliver services in a particular way. You just get comfortable and then some damn fool comes along and changes the playing field.

The pace of change due to technology and the interconnectedness of the world through the Internet is only going to get faster. Years ago, people may have done something in a certain way, oblivious to the fact that another culture had a much easier way to do the same task on the other side of the world. Today, literally minutes after someone finds a new solution, and with one post on social media, and theoretically the whole world can know about it.

Sailors have a term called the WEATHER EYE. It means to keep an eye on the horizon and what weather is heading for your boat.

There is a lot of truth in the fact that a successful marketing business will need to be adaptable to survive in the future. This doesn't mean people will buy insurance in a different way every single day, but the pace of change will speed up, and this will have to be taken into account when working out investments in machines, people, premises or other resources.

It will impact how long you want to sign supply agreements for, it will influence the type of people you employ. It influences a lot of things.

So here's the practical consideration in relation to this habit for survival.

1. Make sure you keep connected to customers so you know what they need and want and how this is changing over time

2. Make sure you don't get 'stuck in your ways' in relation to these changing needs or the changing strategies of your competition or the market

3. Make sure you aren't tied to suppliers who operate on fixed conditions or locking you into contracts – choose adaptable partners too

4. Make sure you hire adaptable staff – those that can handle change as it occurs and don't freeze like a deer in the headlights if you ask them to learn a new app or piece of software

5. Make sure you have business plans, policies, structures in place that support being adaptable as opposed to being fixed to one approach in your market

Simply put it is a market position that is able to be secured and defended. It is the ability of a company to deliver a profitable valuable solution to a specific target audience and have them want to buy it at volumes that will enable the business to prosper.

And it is having the resources available to meet the goals and objectives of the business in relation to delivering that product or service to that target audience.

Business owners who have this TRUTH for their business will survive more effectively and controllably than those who don't

CHAPTER FIVE
A GOAL OR A WISH

CHAPTER FIVE - A GOAL OR A WISH

When push comes to shove, the difference between a goal and a wish is action.

A wish is something you desire or hope for.

A wish is something we generally expect to just magically appear. In fact, many a children's fairy tale presents the idea of 'wishing on a star' or 'putting coins in a fountain' or 'blowing out a candle'

There is absolutely nothing wrong with wishes. They are generally about good things. It is nice to send someone good wishes, to care about their future being bright and cheerful.

The world needs more people to wish more people good.

A wish does not however, generally contain the concept of having to do something to achieve it or to make it happen.

And there lies the crux of the difference between a wish and a goal.

Setting a goal is about really putting a definition around something you want to achieve. And by really putting some thought into defining it, we make the possibility of achieving it more real to ourselves. And we also describe what it will be like when we do achieve it.

And this is an incredibly important step in strategic thinking. It is the most important first step, although not necessarily THE most important step overall.

What I mean is there is no point even trying to start a strategic plan or to work out the steps you need to take until you have clearly defined the end point of the journey. What it looks like, feels like, smells like and so forth.

Setting a goal is exactly like anchoring the other end of a rope you are about to climb. It is exactly like planting a virtual flag at the top of a mountain you are about to ascend. It is exactly like putting a big sign at the end of a road you are about to travel down, perhaps with road signs giving you distance still to travel.

You have to know where in space and time that location is. You have to know what that location looks like. And you have to know what condition you and your business will be in at the moment of your arrival. Let's talk then about some of the factors you should include in goal setting and how you might go about it

CHAPTER SIX
THE 8 BUSINESS ROOMS

Red-G's Steps to Success

Have a long neck

Eat where no one else can eat

Stand tall

When there is no food around, move on

My 3 rooms are the walking room, the eating room and the bathroom

CHAPTER SIX - THE 8 BUSINESS ROOMS

After surveying more than ten thousand business owners - possibly the largest survey of business challenges ever undertaken in Australia, I've been able to identify the 8 key areas in business where busines owners face their biggest challenges.

I used these challenges to reverse engineer a course with 8 steps to being successful in any business.

What sets these 8 steps apart from the usual theoretical course in running a business is they are based on the real-life problems that businesses have. And on the input of 10000 real-life business owners.

We refer to these 8 steps as 'Rooms' in your business.

You have to go into these rooms - setting up systems, doing the work, assigning jobs to team members related specifically to each room in order to be a success as a business owner.

It is interesting that it doesn't matter if your business is one person or a multinational with tens of thousands of employees, these 8 rooms still exist.

Businesses that fail have failed to do the work required in that room - often because they were focussing on just one room to the detriment of all others.

I'm going to spend some time on each room here, to give you some context and ideas for the 8 areas in your business where you can apply strategic thinking and planning.

You can set goals and achieve them in any one of these rooms and therefore collectively across your whole business.

You might have an overall goal and plan for your business, made up of 8 smaller goals or sub-goals and plans for each room.

The beauty of thinking of these 8 success steps as rooms, is you can get the picture of a physical location where you perform these actions. Whilst in this 'virtual' room, you can focus on performing just those actions, and not get distracted by things happening in other rooms.

I'll reinforce this idea as we go along but just to remind you that if you don't go into these rooms on a regular basis, and do the things that are needed in those rooms, you will encounter trouble related to that room.

How do I know that? Because 10000 business owners told me that they encounter these problems from time to time.

And these are the only areas they encounter issues in - or should I say - ALL business issues exist in one of these 8 rooms.

Without further ado, let me share what the 8 rooms are:

1. The Strategy and Leadership Room
2. The Marketing & PR Room
3. The Sales & Business Development Room
4. The Managing Money Room
5. The Managing People Room
6. The Client Service Room
7. The Managing Quality Room
8. The Adapting to Change Room

Now let's look at each room in some detail.

1. THE STRATEGY AND LEADERSHIP ROOM

In the Strategy and Leadership room, your work and effort is directed at strategy, strategic planning, and with the concept of leading others along the journey that your business is taking.

Of course this book is all about strategy and strategic planning, and yes it is a book that you would most likely find in this first and probably most important room in your business.

There is no doubt in my mind - no doubt whatsoever - that you have a better chance of survival and success in your business if you have good plans in place and if you can get others to join you on your journey.

It is a rare business that can survive for long jumping from one day to the next with no plan in mind. Where the owner has to react to problems and is constantly fighting fires.

When entering this room - virtual or not - in your business, you are taking time to plan ahead, to research your market, and to think about what resources you are going to need to run the business for the next significant period of time - months to years in the future.

You are also identifying the key people you need in your corner for the journey that you have mapped out in your strategic plan.

This might be your investors, or your business partner, or your wife, or even your bank manager or accountant.

You are concerned with plans, and you are concerned with communicating with these key people and getting them inspired to help you achieve your goals.

2. THE MARKETING AND PR ROOM

Marketing and Public Relations is another topic of frustration and confusion amongst business owners. Like business plans, we have found that well written and executed marketing plans are pretty rare in business.

It is no surprise that upwards of 30% of all businesses we have surveyed in the last ten years nominate marketing or 'getting new customers' as the biggest challenge they face in business.

In this room, you are concerned with your market and customers and competition and how you as a business owner are going to connect your business and its products and services to those customers or prospects. Marketing is all about making a somewhat uniquely human connection between someone with a product or service, and someone who needs it. And the exchange of money or something else of value for the provision of that product or service.

In this room, some of the activities you are conducting are:

- surveys of prospects and clients on what they need or want along with their behaviours and attitudes towards the type of product or service you offer

- identifying markets for new products and services that people don't even know they need or want, but that satisfy or solve a problem better than anything that came before

- working out what channels of communication you can use to reach the customers you need and want

- getting public relations or what we term - 'other people talking about you' for your company - this is things like word of mouth, local press articles, or even a TV interview for your business

- measuring the results of your marketing programs to see what works best

- to have new customers reaching for the products or services of your business.

3. THE SALES AND BUSINESS DEVELOPMENT ROOM

Whilst the marketing room is all about reaching out to groups of your ideal customer or target audience, the sales room is all about closing deals, or converting the leads that marketing generates.

For your business, this might be a very quick cycle. You do some marketing for lawn mowing using letterbox drops. Someone calls and wants their lawn mowed. You don't really have to sell them as the price was already on the leaflet and all you have to do is book them in, take payment and go and mow the lawn.

Sometimes, it can be a longer cycle. In my business, it may take a few weeks to go from the initial conversation with a potential client, to a meeting, to a proposal or scope of works, to a signed proposal and then delivery of a marketing plan or a business plan or workshop.

In any event, the sales room is all about the process of interacting with one prospect or lead at a time, and signing them up for your product or service. Again, sometimes this sale will be very quick, or may even be done in an 'automated' fashion by your online e-commerce shop.

But the 'sell' still has to be done.

A sale will only occur in your business if the following actions are put in:

- there is a place for the prospect to go, call or visit once they have seen your marketing and have decided they are interested, want to find out more, or want to buy

- there is a process for them to share their needs and wants with your business your staff and yourself
  a process or skill of understanding their needs and wants and how your product or service might satisfy or meet those needs
- the prospect is able to find out about the product or service - the price, what they will receive, how long it will take, your promises and warranties - this may involve a brochure, or it may involve you telling them about it.

- there is a process for ensuring their objections or questions are handled prior to purchase

- there is some process for handling the transaction once they have decided to buy(this might be handed to accounts or treasury in your business and not handled by the salesperson at all)

- there is a process for reversing or cancelling the sale if they change their mind (or policies on refunds, changes etc disclosed at purchase)

- there is a clear process or path for them getting the product or service

- there is a process for handling praise, complaints - google reviews, internal complaints email, forms, in person etc

- there is a process of asking for referrals if they are delighted with our work - referral program, referral vouchers, incentives etc

- there is a process once the sale is completed, for the sales person to hand the client to the team who will organise payment and then subsequently to the team who will deliver the product or service(all with updates to the client on progress if there is a time delay between purchase and receipt of goods/service)

Along with all processes discussed above, there are also processes surrounding the actual way you go about selling which need to be handled in this room. Over time, you might find successful methods of selling, which would all be put in policies and procedures documents and training manuals for new salespeople.

You can probably see that this room is going to be one of the most important rooms in your business. And you can probably also see by now, some or all of the problems that a business owner might have if they haven't spent time developing systems, processes and successful methods in this room.

4. THE MANAGING MONEY ROOM

If there was another part of business that caused the most trouble for business owners, it would be in the money room.

Once again, in our surveys of over ten thousand business owners, money is probably most often the first or second most common source of trouble.

When you enter the money room, you are entering the energy source of all businesses. You simply cannot run a business if you are not generating flows of money into your business, and keeping good control over the recording and reporting of the money and of the money your business spends.

In actual fact, the marketing room and the money room are the most common source of problems, and they are often very closely linked for more than one reason.

Often, the money room is thought to be the source of the problem - i.e not enough money!, but often it can be because the marketing room has troubles which have passed downstream to the money room.

Problems like not pricing the product at the right level to allow for enough profit to run the business. Or perhaps attracting customers who cost a lot in time and money to 'service' reducing the profit on transactions with those clients.

In any event, let's not overcomplicate discussion on the money room. Instead let's look at some of the activities you are conducting when you enter this room.

These activities include:

- invoicing customers
- collecting payments from customers
- opening and reconciling bank accounts of the business
- preparing reports for tax and accounting purposes
- receiving and logging invoices from suppliers
- approving purchases of items needed to run the business
- paying suppliers
- preparing reports for management on the revenue and expenses of the business for an agreed period of time
- ensuring tax obligations are met
- administration and filing of all these reports

In my experience there are a number of specific areas or challenges that business owners run into. These are aligned to the activities above and caused by one of more of these actions being done incorrectly or at the wrong time.

- not invoicing in a timely manner
- not collecting money on time from clients
- making mistakes on invoices
- not having the right bank accounts
- not setting aside money for tax or super
- not setting aside reserves or 'rainy day' money
- inappropriate or uncontrolled expenditure
- poor reporting or recording of money flows
- not keeping up with obligations - super and tax being the most common

5. THE MANAGING PEOPLE ROOM

When we come to the people room, I don't want you to ignore the topic of people just because you don't employ staff.

Managing people isn't just about the people that work for you.

It is also about anyone you rely on to help you run your business - this could be your book keeper, your accountant, your suppliers, your bank manager.

The management of people is often a source of trouble for business owners - small and large.

Anytime you have to co-ordinate the actions of a group of people, it can be complex. Everyone has their own viewpoint on life, their own experiences, their own set of skills, and their own opinions and attitudes.

Aligning these into the one direction, or narrow path you want to tread on your journey, can be a hassle.

But it is possible, if like all the other rooms, you invest the time and energy into working out some straightforward details.

These include:

- who is on this journey with me?
- what am I asking them to do?
- what skills do they have?
- what skills do they need?
- how am I going to keep them up to date on how they are doing at performing the role i've asked them to do?
- how am I going to co-ordinate their activities?
- what laws or rules do I have to abide by in dealing with these people?
- how am I remunerating them for their work?

Over the years, I've experienced some beautiful uplifting moments in running my business with the people on that journey with me. And I've experienced the dark days and depths of despair of working with people too. On our tenth anniversary of our business, we inducted three of our long term clients as honorary team members.

We had an early evening catered event at our offices, with music, great food and invited our staff, their partners and our clients.

We had some informal speeches acknowledging various people who had helped us reach that milestone, which included a plaque presented to those two clients who had been so much a part of our success.

It was a lovely moment for me to acknowledge staff and these clients, but even more uplifting was the responses from those clients on the night. They spoke about the relationship their businesses had with our team and how we were a part of their success too.

It is moments like that which can make running a business like ours so worthwhile.

Another was an event we ran for a client and their community partners. I had devised and developed a highly successful community program for this client.

After a year, we had invited all the community groups - football clubs, schools and other charities to a night where we acknowledged them, presented sponsorship cheques and also awarded members of the community groups for their work in that group - the winners being nominated by the group themselves.

It is a rare moment when you see community volunteers in tears for receiving an award from a single small business, but on that special night there was a real emotional bond created between that business, their staff, the community.

And it would not have been possible without our team creating the program and the opportunity for that company to give back to the community - and grow their business at the same time. Over the two decades of running our business, we've surveyed tens of thousands of businesses and worked closely with over 500 small, medium and large businesses - who collectively have hundreds of thousands of employees.

The key areas of challenge within the People room that I've observed in that time are closely aligned to the activities mentioned above and they include:

- business owners not clearly communicating (in writing) what they need people to do (in other words the absence of job descriptions and measures of performance)
- business owners not giving these individuals an under standing of how their role fits into the overall goals and direction of the business
- business owners not communicating to these people regularly how they are doing in that role

- business owners not understanding, nor complying with laws on how they deal with people

- business owners not realising they should engage and communicate with suppliers and other business partners in the same way as they might engage staff - in other words being clear on the role of the supplier or the partner (supply agreements, briefs, job descriptions)

It might seem at times like all these actions and processes and systems and policies and activity are far too much detail or work to put into these rooms.

On the contrary.

First, the work doesn't have to take a lot of time, and need not be overly complex. For instance a job description can be written on one page.

Secondly, the work done in planning, will avoid 10x or even 100x the work you'll have to do if mistakes are made, or you have to react to problems or issues, or remake products and services, or any number of other cycles you'll have to do if planning is not done first.

90% of running a business, just like painting, is in the preparation. If the preparation is done well, the running of a business should be - no - WILL BE much easier for you.

6. THE CLIENT SERVICE ROOM

If there was a room in our 8 rooms that was most understood and best served by businesses in our surveys it would be the client room.

This is the working IN THE BUSINESS room for your business.

It is the engine room where products and services are scheduled, made and delivered to your clients.

Of course, this room looks very different from business to business.

In my business, it consists of a computer, a conferencing call system, a phone, some processes and strategic tools and perhaps a note pad - along with my experience and wisdom as a consultant.

In a sandwich business, it might consist of a fridge, a preparation space, a counter display area, some signage, knives, cutting board and sandwich fillings and ingredients. Along with loaves of bread and some skilled sandwich making staff.

The reason we call this the working 'IN THE BUSINESS' room is it is the room where most business owners - especially small businesses - get stuck.

Servicing the client - leaving no time for the other rooms.

Many, if not all surviving business owners, are pretty good at delivering the technical aspects of their product or service - when they have a customer to deal with.

For this reason, I'm not going to go into too much detail or give too much advice about this room. After all, you are far more qualified to talk about the products and services of your business than I am.

What I will talk about is how this connects to other rooms, and why those others rooms deserve your attention to make life in this room even easier for you.

Here's some examples of connections:

1. If the marketing room attracts the wrong type of client, your activities in the client room will become more difficult, more time consuming and less successful.

2. If the money room has collected payment, you could be servicing a client who never pays you for your work

3. If someone in this room doesn't do their job, you're going to have to spend more time in the quality room fixing problems.

4. If in the strategy room, you didn't plan for the expansion in number of clients(or a decline) then you might be left with too little or too many resources available for servicing the clients in this room

There are literally hundreds of connections between rooms - some obvious and some not.

Which is why we say that doing all you can across all 8 rooms is the key to being a super successful business owner. No matter how large or small a business you want to run.

7. THE MANAGING QUALITY ROOM

Marketing doesn't grow business over time. Marketing can attract clients to a business, but if the business doesn't deliver on it's promises, it will not survive for long. The reason is that gaining new clients is incredibly expensive compared to keeping those clients and getting word of mouth or a 'reputation' for delivering on your promises.

And quality is all about delivering on promises. If you've ever ordered a product online and then been disappointed when it arrives, you will know what I mean.

You can have all the glossy brochures you like, taken at the best possible angle and in the best possible light. But if the real product doesn't match what it says in the brochure, your business is headed for trouble.

It is no surprise then that when you are in this room, you are concerning yourself with three key things:

1. The standard of quality you have decided to promise to your customers - remember that a pen has a basic standard of quality - it should write - which is distinct from other things - so that a Bic Pen and a Mont Blanc pen are both made in France, but they promise two very different levels of quality.

2. If the standard of quality is being met, time and again by your business - this might be batch to batch on a product, or it might be a written standard or promise in relation to a service.

3. The correcting of production and people when quality of a specific product or service does not meet your own standards or the expectations of your customer.

8. THE ADAPTING TO CHANGE ROOM

By now, anyone who was alive and awake on this planet in early 2020 would understand the need to adapt to change.

More of us are working more from home than anyone could have imagined just 18 months ago, or working in a hybrid arrangement with some time at home and in the workplace.

More businesses are being run from virtual locations than ever before.

More people are buying online.

More children were being schooled at home.

This pandemic has wrought more change in a few short months than most of us witness in a lifetime.

Yet, even in the absence of a pandemic and putting that subject aside for now, most markets and businesses experience change over time.

In the past 40 years, we've moved from tapes and vinyl to CD's to streaming music.

Some of the activities in this room that you might be involved in could include:

- watching trends happening in your market
- observing any new activities by your competition
- keeping an eye on changing needs and wants of customers
- new product development
- new service development
- piloting new ways of doing business (like online selling if you've always sold only from a bricks and mortar location)
- keeping an eye out for any new government legislation, laws, or economic changes that might increase or decrease demand for your product or service

CHAPTER SEVEN
DESCRIBING A GOAL

CHAPTER SEVEN - DESCRIBING A GOAL

In 1981, the first mobile call in Australia was made between Telecom executives. Just over a decade later, the launch of the smartphone saw a supposedly unstoppable market leader - Nokia - get completely swamped by Apple in a few short years.

The bypass of towns on the Pacific highway between Sydney and Queensland, cut 2 and half hours off the journey to Brisbane, but irreversibly changed the business for hundreds of small businesses - including roadside diners, hotels and petrol stations.

In the Adapting to Change Room you should be concerned with activities around predicting and adapting to the changes that can and will occur in the market in which you operate.

Whether these are international changes in the market - such as the move from mere mobile phones to smart phones. Or much more local changes like the diversion of a road around your town.

They might be the arrival of a new competitor in your street, or a new technology to support the delivery of your product or service.

Change might simply be the loss of a top performing staff member from your business.

Wherever change comes from, any business needs to have a method or approach to predicting this change and to dealing with it.

Whilst the main purpose of this book is to help business owners, it is hopefully equally valuable for any individual who wants to set and achieve a goal in some area of their life. From writing a song, to playing an instrument. From learning how to take a photograph, to cooking a meal.

I've used these methods in work and in life.

My main passion in life is to work with and help business owners.

And my hope is that you the reader can use it in your life too.

When I set goals, I like to put as much detail into the description of that goal as I can, so that it not only becomes real to me. But also so that I have an understanding of what it will look like when I reach it.

So I'll always prefer a goal that contains a lot of information, not just a single factor.

Rather than saying - I want to grow my business to $1 million in sales. I would rather state it like this.

To grow our business to a level where we have helped at least 20 clients this year with their strategic planning. Those twenty clients will have delivered on average around $50,000 in revenue, and as a result of helping them, we have reached a turnover of $1million dollars. Our team will consist of 4 highly trained staff who work together in an effective and enjoyable manner. Our clients have all reached their goals and we have achieved high ratings from them for our work, ensuring our future revenue pipeline is also strong.

Without belabouring the point, you can see the second goal gives some really specific detail about what it looks like to have achieved our major goal of revenue. It shows how, with who and also what our business looks like when it has been reached as well as describing how we go about it.

Too detailed? Not for me!

When you describe your goals, use as much detail as is needed for you to feel like it is achievable, real and also enough to describe what it will be like.

Why is the 'what it will be like' component important.

Here's why.

Do you recall in old newspapers there was a game called 'spot the difference'?

Well in that game there were two pictures, with hidden and slight changes in each picture. You had to find 5, 10 or maybe 15 differences. It was an exercise in observation.

I find this analogy very useful in both goal setting and strategy because a well described future situation allows you to compare your business today with that intended future. You'll see the differences between what you want it to be, and how it is, and gradually as you get closer to your goal, the current picture and the future picture will start to look the same.

I recall a time when I did this for our business. I wrote down our goal which included references to a busy office, with the noise of productive staff servicing our clients and the smell of freshly roasted coffee and delicious organic food from our own 'inside-the-business' cafe.
One day I was sitting at my desk reviewing our goals and plans, and I looked up and saw the busy office, the noise of productive staff servicing our clients. The only thing that was missing was the cafe, and then I realised we were located right above a cafe of that exact description - the only difference was we didn't own it.

But it was in the same location as our office.

How about that?

It was an amazing moment of recognition that describing your goals in great detail, can help you recognise when you've reached your goals.

And also that the enjoyment of reaching the goal is about more than the revenue or the profit.

Is there a difference between personal and business goals?

Whilst the subject matter of the goal might be different, the process is pretty much the same.

It isn't a matter of just arbitrarily stating a goal in a few seconds and writing it down.

It is and should be a little bit more involved.

A goal should be real to you, and also doable.

There is nothing wrong with having big goals. I'm not trying to squash anyone's dreams here.

But if you write for example that you want to be standing on the surface of Mars one year from now, it would not be possible. For one thing, you might not be a billionaire.

For another, you might not be physically able to travel into space.

But beyond all that, the trip to Mars is two years long with current space technology. So even if everything lined up, you would have had to leave a year ago to reach that goal.

You might think that this is an extreme example, but I can tell you that many of the goals that I hear business owners express are no less impossible to achieve. They almost always overestimate the size of where they want to be and underestimate the resources and effort to get there.

We, unfortunately, live in a world where people and businesses want more than they can have with the effort or money they are willing to put into things.

We are constantly sold the idea of something for nothing, the magic bullet.

We are sold the 'gambler's model' of life.

In my experience, and I think in yours too - if you are honest about it - the rewards actually go mostly to those who work for it.

Sure, there might be examples of the 'overnight' success, or the instant billionaire, sold in the media. But we don't really believe it, do we?

And even if we did, they are as rare as hen's teeth or rocking horse poo.

So I'd like to have an agreement with you about the contents and topic of this book.

Myself as the author and you as the reader agreeing that something worthwhile will take some skill, effort and investment of time and money to achieve.

I think for the bulk of the population, and the bulk of businesses out there, that this is going to be a much more workable approach to life.

This is the path I follow. I believe I'll get more if I give more.

I'll get revenue if I exchange high-value services with my customers. I don't want to get something for nothing.

And I don't think you want to either. If you do, maybe this book isn't for you.

So how do you set goals?

CHAPTER EIGHT
SETTING OF GOALS

Red-G's guide to goal setting

Decide where you want to go

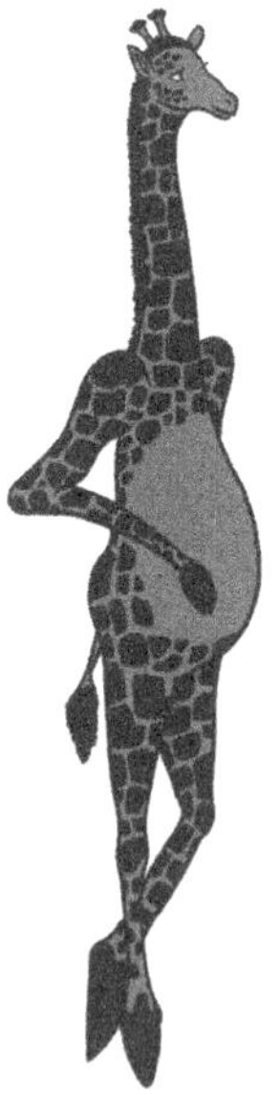

Get ready to go there

Go there

Repeat

CHAPTER EIGHT - SETTING OF GOALS

It is a natural first step in goal setting to plant a virtual 'flag' somewhere or sometime in the future, that indicates the desired end of your journey.

At this flag's location is the description of your goal, in all its glory. As discussed in the previous pages.

It is an exciting moment to define what you are aiming for, and where and when you want that aim to be realised.

I have developed an approach to setting goals that I've found to be workable in my business.

1. I first look at the current situation our business is in, in relation to the specific goal I want to set. If it is a revenue goal, then I look at current revenues. If it is a goal on other parameters, for instance writing a book, it might be the size of the book and the date I'd like to publish it.

2. I then analyse and observe what has made up that current situation - how many clients contributed to the overall result? Where did we get those clients? What did we do for that revenue? What is the current status of my book idea?

3. Then and only then will I consider what might be possible in the timeframe for when I'm setting the next goal. Most of the time I'm setting either a goal for the next 12 months or perhaps a shorter cycle like the next quarter. For a book project, it will be for a specific date in time.

4. I then write a goal that is within the realms of possibility but big enough to be exciting and a little challenging - I don't want it to be easy. I want to reach the target just in time for the bell to ring on the last day of the target due date. And to reach it out of breath like I've run the last kilometre in world record time for my age.

If you are working with a team in your business, then I'd suggest the following additional steps.

5. In looking at the current situation, be sure you include enough specifics for your team to understand the situation, and also their place in it.

6. Break down the review of the actions that it took getting to the current situation into the areas each person is responsible for. You want them to start feeling involved in the process from here on out.

7. Ask each person their viewpoint on what is possible in the next target period in their role and overall. Listen to their ideas, and note any barriers or objections they discuss. These will be important later on.

8. When you set a goal, make sure it is one that everyone can buy into. Yet again, don't let them talk you out of a goal that stretches everyone to the limits of their skill and ability. In this section, you'll also want to make sure you've handled any considerations or concerns the team might have. But what if we don't have the resources? What if we don't get the clients?Will I be under the pump? Do it in a positive way, still stretch them, but don't leave them hanging by being un real about what they will have to do, don't expect twice the result from the same investment of time and effort. And don't be a slave driver or obnoxious about it either.

CHAPTER NINE
STRATEGY-MEANING

CHAPTER NINE - STRATEGY - MEANING

The word itself has a simple meaning - it comes from the greek 'strategos' which means to lead an army or literally 'generalship'.

The modern definition in military terms is the art of planning and directing overall military operations and movements in a war or battle. The modern business definition is a plan of action designed to achieve a long-term or overall aim. But people can and do get tied up in knots thinking about the complexity of strategy.

Some people have been known to go ashen white when asked to develop a strategy for a business or some other activity. It conjures up weighty documents that spend years on the shelf gathering dust.

Strategy can feel like being forced to a listen to a boring professor of a subject you can't even spell, let alone understand. This reaction is understandable. But that is not the way it is supposed to be.

In essence, the use of strategy should just match the meaning of the bright ideas and actions put in place by someone to reach a goal. It should inspire you.

So in that vein, let's look at some of the tools you can use. And rather than get too serious about the tool itself, let's also look at why they were invented. I hope you'll discover along the way that in fact all strategic tools were designed to make life simpler for the business owner - not more complex. They were designed to help you understand things better, not make them worse.

Where did we go wrong from design to execution of these tools?

We forgot what they were designed for, and instead starting reading too much significance into the process of filling out forms, and ticking boxes and the administration of them.

I hope to re-inspire you with the truth about the origins of these tools, and have you realise that as tools, they are there to be used, and there to make your task easier - just like a shovel makes digging a hole a lot easier than doing it with your hands.

CHAPTER TEN
STRATEGY VERSUS TACTICS

The main difference between strategy and tactics is that one is generally longer term and the other is short term. A tactic can be part of a strategy. A strategy cannot be part of, or subservient to a tactic.

In other words, a strategy helps you design a tactic. It should never be the other way around.

In any one business, operating in any one market, serving any one type of customer, there are literally millions of tactical actions you can take in that business to promote to, attract and service customers.

However, not all these tactics are the same. Some take more time, some take more money.

In business, you have to be efficient. You have to deploy the optimum amount of time, money and energy to attract each client. That amount of time, money and energy needs to be less than the profit or margin on your product or you will go out of business fast.

You have to use strategy to inform tactics.

Strategy is the head, tactics are the feet.

Don't just run about in circles.

Plan it with thought using your head, then decide which direction to run and how fast. Do it the other way, letting the feet be in charge is a recipe for disaster.

However, many businesses don't operate like this. They work in an ad-hoc reactive fashion. A problem comes up, they try and fix it, it comes up again they fix it again. They never stop and think, hey that problem has come up a few times - let's work out a way to avoid making it.

Strategy literally is the planned actions you take, measuring the effectiveness and efficiency of each as you go, so you can get to your destination with exactly the right amount of time, money and energy invested.

It is how you stay in business.

It is how you beat your competition.

It is how you know what your customers need, and how you are going to serve them.

Tactics have no right to be in charge of things around here.

You need to use strategy to keep order in your business.

Here's a few examples to reinforce this point.

PIZZA SHOP

Imagine you had $1000 to spend on a marketing campaign for your new Pizza Shop. Where would you spend it?

My approach would be to pick say 3 things to trial. Spend $300 on each and see what works best. Then when you get your next $1000 for marketing, you can spend the $1000 on the most successful idea from the first trial.

So you might print some leaflets and drop them in some local letterboxes with your first $300. You might make some pizzas and pay a staff member $300 to stand out the front of the shop offering some trial 'taste tests', and for the last $300, you spend $50 a day for 6 days on Facebook Advertising to people in your local suburb online.

You find that the most successful return for your investment was doing the sample taste test as you sold 10 Pizzas to those people. 5 came in with leaflets from your letterbox drop and no-one came in mentioning the special on facebook. You see, next time you can pay a staff member $1000 to stand out there for longer and you'll sell more Pizzas.

RECYCLING BUSINESS

You decide you are going to start a business making things out of recycled plastic.

You buy a machine kit online that helps you melt and form old milk bottles into flower pots.

You advertise these and don't get any takers. No sales, despite all your investment, and your passion for recycling.

What could you do as a strategic action to get sales?

One way would be to find out in your local area if there were any gardening clubs, or nurseries that could stock your product. Or you might find out if there was a group who were promoting recycling in your local area.

Research is a strategic action that should be done to find out if a business idea is viable BEFORE you invest in equipment and manufacturing and promotion.

CONSULTING BUSINESS

A friend had a business providing consulting to his clients. He employed quite a few staff and things were going well. However, there was an economic recession and he lost some clients. Now he had too many employees and his costs were high and he went out of business.

A strategic action he could have taken was to move to outsource work to his staff and make them contractors instead of staff.

In this way, he would have moved a fixed cost in his business outside the business and ups and downs in client revenue would have less impact on him. If things got quiet he could always do the work himself until he had enough to outsource. And even if sales went down he didn't have all the fixed costs sitting there.

This is strategic planning. Working out the right business model for a business. Working out the right marketing. Working out what customers need.

CHAPTER ELEVEN
PLANNING VERSUS ACTION

There is a big difference between planning and action.

Planning is a contemplative process. It is about research, and weighing up options. Looking at trends, and considering scenarios.

Action is well, active.

It is motion, getting things started and completed.

It's about communicating to your market, handling reaches from prospects, meeting with clients, and servicing their needs.

The relationship between planning and action, is the same as the relationship between strategy and tactics.

Planning informs action. Action doesn't inform planning.

The beauty of the two is revealed in actions that are well planned as they are actions which will give you the most reward for your effort.

If an action doesn't work, you don't keep trying to do it, expecting some sort of magic to occur. You check your planning, refine it, and then act again.

If you are ever confused about what to do, my recommendation is to come up with a strategy, or a plan, based on careful consideration and contemplation, and then act.

While it is certainly fun to be spontaneous. And certain things in business can be all about spontaneity, I definitely know from my experience that planned actions in business are far more likely to succeed and succeed earlier and with better results than unplanned chaos.

Whilst we are on the topic of action, I'd like to share the importance of constant and regular progress towards your goals.

Big goals are more easily attained when they are broken down in smaller and smaller parts that can be completed one at a time - thus eventually reaching the whole of the goal.

I wrote an article on that a few years back called 365 days of action and I'm including it here for you:

365 DAYS OF ACTION - *originally published on Linkedin in July 2016.*

I like to think of 'action' in the context of the Indian Proverb about the Elephant, "How do you eat one? One bite at a time!"

The best way to achieve a big goal is to do something towards that goal every single day of the year. With 365 days of action, you'll be much more likely to get to your goals more often.

Imagine you decided to walk the Camino in Spain. Initially the journey would seem huge - walking 40 kilometres a day for 40 days in a row!

But break it down day by day, and then hour by hour and soon you come to something that you can confront - I need to walk 4 kilometres in the next hour - you get the idea!

And the same goes for your strategic plan. A great strategic plan isn't one which is beautifully presented with eloquent positioning statements, and well organised tactics - that sits on a shelf! A great plan is all those things and one other important ingredient - action every day.

If you set yourself goals and objectives in a plan - you'll soon find out the only way to achieve them is do something.

If you've planned to hire a new staff member, launch a new product, or start a new marketing campaign it only gets done if you do the small actions that all add up to a completed product or goal reached.

So the next time you write your strategic plan, get yourself organised to work on it daily and soon enough you'll be drinking a nice glass of champagne at the end of your journey.
Sometimes you have to be a pilgrim to be a successful business owner.

It's easy to get distracted and to follow some idea down a rabbit hole.

You must keep an eye on the big picture and on the big goals, and be constantly vigilant that what you are doing each day is contributing to the overall plan.

It is indeed a rare skill to project a certain goal out into an uncertain future and then put in place the plans and activity to bring it to reality.

To actually pull it off regularly, will make you seem like part time traveller and part magician to others who will look at your ability to get things done with awe.

But in reality, it isn't magic; it is more like a mix of inspiration and perspiration.

DISCIPLINE IS ALSO IMPORTANT

If you've broken down big goals into smaller parts and you are working on them regularly, the other area that is important to focus on is discipline. You need to keep ensuring that your daily, weekly and monthly tasks are the right ones, and that you avoid as much as possible being dragged down rabbit holes of things you don't need to be doing.

There is absolutely nothing wrong with taking a break every now and then, but if you spend your days being 'busy' but not really completing the actions that contribute to the overall goal, you will run into trouble.

You'll only have yourself to blame if you don't then reach your goals in the timeframe you've set yourself.

I'm deliberately being tough on you here - but there is no place for being a victim when it comes to setting goals and working on strategy.

You need to act like you are in control, wherever and whenever you can.

Sure things come up that you can't control and maybe here and there you'll get diverted by urgent and important things.

You might have a family issue you need to handle, or a client problem just has to be handled right there and then.

The game is to do the things that matter as much of the time as possible.

Don't waste the times when you have no urgent or important diversions that come up, and then fritter it away with meaningless activity.

It should be fun to be doing the things that help you reach your goals. If they are important to you, even facing barriers and challenges and overcoming them will be enjoyable.

A friend of mine used to say 'it is easier to say NO when you have a bigger YES in mind.

So! What are you waiting for?

CHAPTER TWELVE
THE SCOPE OF A STRATEGY SHOULD MATCH THE SCOPE OF YOUR BUSINESS

CHAPTER TWELVE - THE SCOPE OF A STRATEGY SHOULD MATCH THE SCOPE OF YOUR BUSINESS

When you work on strategic planning, you need to keep the scope of your plans to the real scope of your business operations - current and future.

Don't go off to Mars with ideas, if you are only ever going to operate within one state.

There is a lot of rubbish about anyone being able to operate a global business these days, but generalisations like this can be incredibly dangerous if they are not real.

The fact is, they can't.

There are perfectly good reasons why a grower of fresh flowers can't sell them globally - because the flowers will spoil before they arrive.

Same goes for a hot cup of coffee from your local cafe.

And lawn mowing.

And probably real estate.

And personal in-home care support.

And hundreds of other businesses that I don't have the time or space to mention.

I've hope I've made my point.

Be careful when you are planning a new business, or the growth of an existing one to keep the boundaries of your planning and investment real.

We have a client in Melbourne who has some bricks-and-mortar store locations. What we have discovered is that no matter what we do in terms of advertising or promotion - it is incredibly rare for any customer - trade or retail - to travel more than 15 kilometres to one of their stores.

In other words, there is a virtual travel barrier just like a 10-foot tall electric steel customer-proof fence that encircles each store just about 15 kilometres from that store.

I've heard a similar story repeated by other clients and friends with products and services that people like to experience in person before they buy. Online sales don't work for these products and services for whatever reason.

So for them, there is every point in looking at a new location in an area that doesn't overlap the other stores - perhaps an outer suburb.

But there is no point, in using national magazines to promote their business, because there are a lot of customers reading that magazine that no matter what happens will never travel to their store locations.

The same goes for a restaurant in St Kilda that used to advertise on the radio to all of Melbourne and never got customers from more than 5-10 kilometres away. Or so few in number that the wasted money on promotion - when local advertising was a lot cheaper - just didn't make sense.

There are great products and certain services which can definitely command a global audience.

But don't fall into the trap of assuming you can get to a global audience, if there is an obvious reason why this is not going to be the case for you.

You might be able to grow a global audience, but also remember that this means global advertising, and global logistics and exchange rate variations and a range of other issues that mean you'll have to sell a lot of product to make a similar profit to a smaller, more local business.

Think of the analogy of military supply lines. There was a reason many battles were lost because food, fuel and ammunition couldn't reach far flung troops.

An alternative might be to only sell locally and personally deliver products and make more money.

Of course it all depends on your product and your service. I'm just making a point to not have fixed ideas about what type of business, and the business model you choose.

The same sort of argument goes for selling direct to a few customers, compared to trying to get national distribution in a retail store.

We did this calculation for a client and found they could make the same profit selling just 128 products direct to customers as they would selling 1000 via the chains. This was because of increasing marketing, distribution costs and a lower margin because of the margin the chain wanted for their work in selling your product.

Big is not always better is my cautionary word on strategic planning.

Be big if it makes sense. Be small if it makes sense.

Don't judge yourself or your business on size. That is Ego.

Judge yourself on the ability of your business to generate financial security for yourself, and jobs for your staff, and help for your chosen charity or community, or on being sustainable.

These are far more important than the Ego trip of being global or being seen in a famous store.

Make sure your strategy fits the size you are and the size you can be.

CHAPTER THIRTEEN
STRATEGIC TOOL KIT

Red G'S tool kit

My horns (ossicones) that I use to fight other male giraffes

My tail - that I use to flick flies

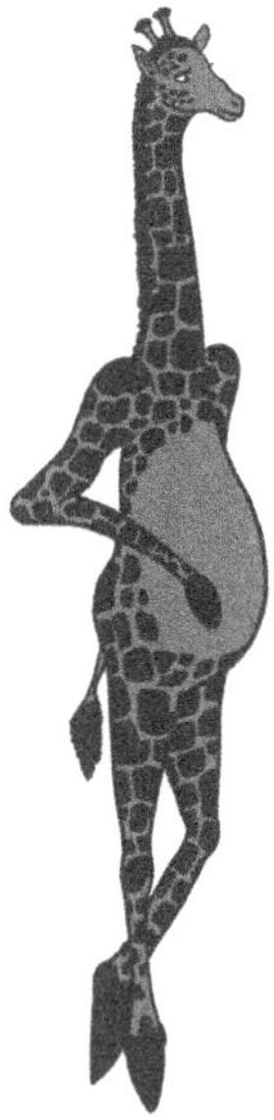

My neck - that I use to neck other giraffes - fancy name eh!

My legs - that I use to run, and by the way, drinking is hard - real hard. I wish my neck was longer or my legs were shorter, because it can be a real bitch getting a drink

In this section of the book, I want to share with you a range of specific strategic tools.

I'm hoping to make these tools much more accessible and useful for you by describing the purpose of the tool as well as how to use it.

You may have heard of some of the tools before. Some you won't because they have been developed by our team, and only used internally with our clients until now.

I think it is a good approach to think of strategic tools just like any other tool. A shovel, hammer, scissors or a hair dryer.

Even though they are made up of words and symbols, and are intangible compared to a shovel, they are tools nonetheless.

They have a purpose, they are to be used.

And you need to use the right tool for the right job.

You may not use all these tools in your strategic plan.

Just choose the ones that make most sense to the business challenge you are trying to solve.

Don't just use them aimlessly, use them to help you achieve the goals you have set, for the personal or business purpose you desire.

SWOT ANALYSIS

I'm sure you've heard of a SWOT Analysis before. SWOT is an acronym that stands for Strengths, Weaknesses, Opportunities and Threats.

The purpose of this tool is to help you work out what you are good at, what you stink at, where you could grow your market or business, and where you might face opposition or risk.

It is an amazing tool, rarely used well.

Often it is done as a box ticking exercise, and not translated into actual strategic actions afterwards.

There is also a significant missing ingredient even when a SWOT is done. That is to match up items in the various 4 boxes, to really give you direction and focus on things to work on in your business.

SWOT ANALYSIS

STRENGTHS *Internal to your company*	**WEAKNESSES** *Internal to your company*
OPPORTUNITIES *External environment*	**THREATS** *External environment*

EXAMPLES OF USING THE SWOT IN ACTION.

1. Let's say you have surveyed customers and they say you are really good at responding to their enquiries. You also find out that potential new prospects also want responsiveness and your competitors are not good at it. Identifying this in your SWOT, you can then focus on promoting how responsive you are to the market.

2. In another example, you find out that your delivery services are poorly rated by customers. Here's an action you can put in place to work out a way to get a better courier, or perhaps buy your own delivery van. It becomes a focussed investment in improving some thing that is holding your business back.

3. What if you find out that a competing business in a neighbouring suburb has gone out of business. You might open a new location to take advantage of that opportunity

PESTLE ANALYSIS

The idea behind most of the famous strategic planning tools has always been to make life easier for the person or company using them. The PESTLE Analysis is no different.

It is another acronym that stands for **P**olitical, **E**conomic, **S**ocial, **T**echnological, **L**egal and **E**nvironmental.

What are these things?

They are simple different areas of the market or environment that might impact your business.

And breaking them up into different boxes, allows you to focus your thinking on each one in turn, and identify if there is a trend there that is important for you to take into account.

TEMPLATE - PESTLE ANALYSIS

Company Name: ______________________________

Date completed: ______________________________

Completed by: ______________________________

TREND CATEGORY	NOTES
Political	
Economic	
Social	
Technology	
Legal	
Environmental	

An economic trend might be say lower interest rates which is going to increase demand for land and houses, and you run a building company so you can identify an opportunity for growth for you.

A political trend might be a change of government and the new party being sworn in isn't as friendly in policy terms to your type of business - so maybe there is a risk of lower sales for the next political term.

What about new laws coming in that require your business to have a specific qualification or certification for your staff. This is a trend that is going to mean you have higher training costs in the future.

A social trend might be people buying more of your product online, meaning you have to invest in a better e-commerce site and better delivery options for those products. The upside is you might be able to decrease investment in your bricks and mortar locations. This recently occurred when Kogan bought the Matt Blanc furniture stores. The new owner closed the stores and took the brand completely online.

An environmental trend might be the desire for customers to have a recycled plastic option for packaging, which means you have to look into different suppliers for your packaging and perhaps change prices depending on these cost changes.

We could provide hundreds of more examples, but I'm sure you get the picture.

That the PESTLE is an enormously valuable tool for identifying and then acting on trends in your market.

COMPETITOR ANALYSIS

In my business - Blue Frog Marketing - we developed our own strategic tool to analyse the competitors of our clients when working on business and marketing plans.

Whilst there are loads of things you can review about your competitors, there are certainly things that are really important:

- their pricing
- how they advertise
- how satisfied their customers are
- how good they are in key factors compared to you
- what they talk about in annual reports (if these are publicly available)
- where they are located
- what their offices or shops look like
- what is their positioning?
- are they always discounting or more of a premium brand?

You don't always have to focus on competitors in your business. But it does pay to keep one eye on what they are doing.

There are a couple of alternative strategies to deal with competitors - you can be a market leaders - in other words come up with your own strategy, your own ideas, your own promotions, your own value proposition - and essentially ignore the competition. Or you can be a follower - in other word, let the other guys and gals make the market moves, and then follow them, or follow them and be just that little bit better.

Sometimes you can be a leader, sometimes you have to be the follower. Both choices carry with them different approaches and different strategies.

Just be careful - as one movie actor once said - that you don't bring a knife to a gunfight.

In other words, if one of your competitors is focusing on being the cheapest and they are big and have lots of resources, it is best not to get into a bidding war with them - because you will lose.

As mentioned elsewhere in this book - a smaller competitor - if that is you - is better served by finding a niche where they can win the battle with a more focused or smaller part of the overall market - an area where you hold some advantages over the bigger player in the market.

MARKET ANALYSIS

Every business should know the current state of the market in which they operate. It doesn't matter whether your customers all come from your local suburb, or even a local market stall. It doesn't matter if you operate across a whole city, or a region, or state or country or globally.

With the boundaries of the market you operate in, it is important for you to have some awareness of what is going on, what factors are important for success in that market, and for you to keep an eye on any changes occurring.

A lack of attention on a market, and you can get surprised. And surprises are the natural enemy of a business owner. In fact surprises - either positive or negative ones - can all be difficult to handle.

Keeping a weather eye on your market (an old sailors term for watching for weather changes on the horizon) is important.

The factors that are useful to include in any market analysis are:

- your location and information about the local economy
- any competitors to you in the area you operate

- any changes/impacts that might increase/decrease customers getting to your location

- any seasonal trends in your area

- any opportunities to promote yourself in the local area - local media as well as any broader media that reaches your area and fits in your budgets

- any government impact on your operations - e.g. permits for outdoor seating in your cafe?

- what businesses or organisations you could partner with any economic news related to your market?

NEEDS AND WANTS ANALYSIS

Essentially the information for needs and wants is identified by surveying your potential customers or customers.

But once data is collected, you need to analyse the information to tease out the most important data for you and your business.

This means:

- what needs are you already good at servicing?

- what needs are there that you are currently poor at servicing.?

- if you are going to service a new need that you identified what is the opportunity and the cost of servicing that - for example if you started offering faster delivery is there an extra benefit in more sales, or are costs going to wipe out any sales increase benefit

- are needs real and will people pay more if that need is satisfied? - it is one thing for someone to want something and another thing to want to pay for it

- are the needs and wants of this potential customer worth planning to service or would you be better targeting another type of customer - different age, different income brackets?

- what are your competitors doing? - if there is no one else able to offer that need or want, is there an opportu nity for you, or will you have some other company who is always going to be better than you. A classic example is trying to out compete a larger business on price or range. Often small businesses make the mistake of competing directly with larger organisations in the same market position. Smaller companies are better to find a niche where they can out compete a larger business on a smaller scale, or for a specific group of customers.

NEW PRODUCT DEVELOPMENT TOOL

I don't think you would be surprised to hear how much wasted time and money goes into the development of products that no one wanted in the first place.

This is all driven by the dreaded mistake of relying on assumptions versus market facts.

Yes, there is a case to be made that people sometimes don't know what they need until they see it. But the strategy of creating a market that doesn't yet exist can be expensive if you don't know what you are doing.

For most businesses, who are not releasing some ground breaking new service, or technology - there is a proven method to new product development and it should include the following steps:

1. A review of your existing product range and identifica tion of what is selling and what isn't

2. If you are launching a new business, a detailed review of what else is available to the market and already serving the market including price, features, feedback and more.

3. A concept survey with customers and potential customers on needs/wants and whether the new offer from that product or service is actually needed and wanted and what people would be prepared to pay for it.

4. A review of competitors locally, and identifying if possible the size of the prize for your new service or product. Are you the 5th cafe to offer a 'gluten free' menu. Is there enough demand to satisfy a new entry.

5. How likely are people to adopt new services/new technology.

6. A cost analysis of the research, production and launch of the new technology or product or service and if it will cannibalise your existing products or services (cannibalise in this context meaning to "take away from")

7. An honest review of your capacity or capability to bring that new service or product to market and make profit from it

8. Some form of milestone process where you can test, measure and decide go or no go at various points of research, trial and investment into the idea

I've seen literally thousands of cases of 'bright-idea's' that someone assumed was going to make millions, which fell in an absolute heap because the company or person didn't really research their idea or didn't really understand the market into which they were launching the idea.

In one classic example that I can share, a company called me in because they were not reaching their sales goals for a product they had developed. Not reaching their goals was probably an overstatement - they had virtually sold none of this product.

When I asked them their launch process, I found out they had invested hundreds of thousands in plant, equipment, molds for their product, and manufacturing. But had not spoken to a single client before making all this investment.

This is the very definition of insane.

Zero research and hundreds of thousands of wasted investment.

In another, I was mentoring an individual who was bringing a new product to Australia that he said was going to sell millions because it was half the cost of the nearest alternative already in the market.

What he failed to find out before investing nearly $30,000 in costs, was that the product was not approved for sale for the use he wanted to promote - and never would be approved due to certain issues with the ingredients and Australian regulation. So much money wasted for want of a little more strategic investigation.

RETURN ON INVESTMENT TOOL

Some years ago, I developed a simple tool to measure the investment in marketing programs for clients.

This simple tool has become one of the most invaluable devices we've ever created, and is used constantly in marketing programs and broader strategic programs.

Essentially is is comprised of

- direct costs(money spent on something)
- indirect costs (time for labour, research, etc - assigned a cost and calculated) these are added up.
- direct return (actual sales generated in real dollars, actual profit generated in actual sales)
- indirect return (new benefits not in actual dollars such as leads, referral partnerships, website visitors, appointments made, media stories generated

Taking the outflow of expenses and effort and comparing it to the inflow of business and other results you can get two measures.

One is the cash ROI - which is a ratio of revenue to costs. We've had programs creating as high as $72 for every $1 invested in marketing.

The other is intangible opportunity ROI - which is all the other inflows which you might not be able to put a dollar figure on, but which can contribute to future revenue or growth of your business. For example, you might sign a partnership deal with someone and they start referring new prospect to you six months down the track.

BRIEFING TOOL

There is a saying a mentor of mine - Glen Carlson of DENT Global - has.

"You get what you pitch for and you are always pitching."

I have a similar saying in relation to briefing projects to suppliers -

"You get back what you brief."

A long time ago I learnt the lesson that a brief must be written down and accompany any communication to someone whom you are asking to do a specific task.

For example a business card or a brochure.

If you write down as much detail as you can about what you are looking for, including a budget, brand colours, customer insights and a range of other things, the person doing the work doesn't have to assume things about the project.

I had a situation where we briefed a website designer and were initially told the total cost would be $4000 to design and build our site. Two days later, the designer delivered twice the pages we asked for and then started demanding double the budgeted amount. Not only that, but they hadn't included the actual build and launch of the site in their response to the brief.

Our brief was titled website design, and there was a miscommunication between our account manager and the designer who thought they had quoted on a price per page for design only and that there was an open chequebook to do as many pages as they thought would meet the brief.

At our end, we wanted a 4-page site - designed and live and available for clients to view. It was a bit of a disaster to be frank, and cost too much money in the end for what was really required.

IDEA GENERATION TOOL

Ideas are an important part of running a business.

Sometimes they come out of the blue when you least expect it - walking the dog, washing the car, doing the shopping.

Sometimes, they can be a little harder to come by. You might have a situation in your business from time to time, when you need the spark of inspiration.

We created a directed way to come up with ideas that we have used regularly and I wanted to share it with you here.

Feel free also to take these ideas, thought starter exercises, and create your own. The great thing about creative idea generation is you can use any context or exercise you like. The sky is the limit.

1. *Technical* - think of some technical features that could represent or solve your problem - a wheel, an engine, a wind up toy, a plane, a kite

2. *Animals* - if you were a camel how would you solve a water storage problem - you'd grow a hump. If you were a beaver you solve the problem of needing calm pool of water in a ranging river - you'd build a dam. Think of an animal and then how they might solve your issue - this can be fun

3. *Colours* - orange is an optimistic colour - if you were optimistic how would you solve this problem. Blue is a calm colour - if you were calm, how would you solve it. It doesn't matter what colour or mood you choose for that colour, this is a fun exercise

4. *Child* - how would a child solve your problem. The greek philosopher Heraclitus said 'man is most nearly himself when he achieves the seriousness of a child at play' - the idea here is to not be serious at all - which us adults are far too often when confronted with a problem. Throw the seriousness out of the window - go crazy and laugh. Another wise person said the haha of laughter is closely related to the a-ha of discovery.

5. *Symbols* - if the problem was represented by a triangle what would the solution be, a circle?, an asterisk?. Pick a symbol and have some fun

6. *Art's and craft* - paint your problem, draw it, make a piece of pottery out of it

This method of choosing a different way of approaching a problem really tap into other avenues of your thinking and abilities that you don't know you have.

Stop sitting there staring into space or moping about the problem, create a game and I guarantee you will come up with other ideas and solutions for what you are trying to fix.

I had a new business problem at my agency, and with that problem in mind I was walking around a stationery store and I saw they had a special on these big brown folders. I grabbed a number of them, took them to my office, and stuck a money value on the front of each. I then took them to my work in progress meeting and created a program called - creatively enough - the 'Brown Bags' new business program. The idea was anyone could grab a bag and create an idea or proposal for an existing client or a new prospective client to the value of that bag.

We then pitched these ideas to our existing clients and prospects and if we won the business, the person who created it got a prize. In the following 3 months, we won 12 of 13 pitches and generated hundred of thousands in new income. All out of about $5 worth of brown bags, a bit of fun, and the creativity of our team. But it took the bright idea to kick it off. It wasn't ground shattering or the best idea ever, but it worked.

Try it for yourself.

DRIVERS/RESTRAINERS ANALYSIS

I use this tool as a simplified alternative to a SWOT Analysis as I found that in certain situations I didn't need that complexity of internal and external factors in analysing a project or opportunity.

This is an elegant and simple tool.

Drivers are defined as anything that is going to help you achieve the result on a certain project.

Restrainers are defined as anything that is going to hinder you in achieving the result.

DRIVERS/RESTRAINERS TEMPLATE

Business Name: ______________________

Date: ______________________

COMPONENT	NOTES/ACTIONS
Drivers - things that will contribute/help to us reaching our goals.	*Ways to strengthen or protect drivers*
Drivers - things that will contribute/help to us reaching our goals.	*Ways to avoid, get over, deal with restrainers, or ignore if not massive impact on business*

EXAMPLE: OVER 50'S GYMNASIUM

COMPONENT	NOTES/ACTIONS
Drivers - things that will contribute/help to us reaching our goals. *Ageing Population* *Older bodies subject to more injuries* *No other gyms focus-sing on this age group*	*Ways to strengthen or protect drivers* *Publish content on ageing population and 50_ injuries* *Publish a self help book and become known as expert.* *Name ourselves in a way that 50+ people are inspired to come to us.*
Drivers - things that will contribute/help to us reaching our goals. *Poor economy mean-ing people less likely to use a gym.* *Over 50's go to a doctor or use a muscle rub and do it themselves.* *Another gym deciding to compete in our age group.*	*Ways to avoid, get over, deal with restrainers, or ignore if not massive impact on business* *Get our gym services listed on medicare* *Partner with doctors* *Cross promotion with a muscle rub company* *Offer better value and better pro-grams than competition and under-stand this age group better.*

Once you've spent some time thinking about these two factors, you can then put in place very specific actions to take advantage of the drivers, and to do something to handle, block, or avoid the restrainers.

We find this tool to be nice and simple, yet a powerful way to plan for an upcoming project and to see it from all sides. Both the opportunity and the risk. Some examples of drivers might be - a change in customers, referral from existing customers, finding a new location for your business, pitching for new business in a tender

Some example of restrainers might be - loss of a skilled salesperson, a lockdown due to pandemic, lack of resources to invest in marketing, an unhappy customer giving you a poor rating online which influences others. Parts or supplies not arriving so you can finish orders.

UP/DOWN ANALYSIS

Another fantastic yet simple tool we pioneered is the up/down analysis.

We've used this particularly with clients who have a lot of ongoing clients like trade customers, or B2B businesses.

You use this tool in this way:

1. Gather a list of your top 100 customers for this year.

2. Do the same for the previous year

3. Make sure you are using a similar period of time - last 12 months sales, last 3 months versus previous 3 months

4. Note all customers who have increased their purchases(the up's) and all customers who have decreased purchases(the down's)

You can review each customer and determine what occurred for each of these changes.

A survey of any customers who have stopped or slowed purchases is a good idea. It also makes a good reason to reach out and call the customer.

Sometimes you might find it is something that has impacted their business or it might be something you or your team did to influence that change.

Either way it is a useful indicator and a great way to focus your mind on opportunities and risks in the sales area.

For example, what if you found that a long term customer stopped buying because of your slow deliveries, you might be able to get them back if you fix the issue. Or what if you found from a customer that one of your competitors was out of stock on a critical product, and you were the only nearby supplier. This might prompt you to take that information and then use it to promote to all customers and rally up even more business for yourself.

UP/DOWN TEMPLATE

Business Name: ______________________

Date: ______________________

COMPONENT	NOTES
Customer 1	*Up 5%*
Customer 2	*Up 5%*
Customer 3	*Up 5%*
Customer 4	*Up 5%*
Customer 5	*Down 5%*
Customer 6	*Down 5%*
Customer 7	*Down 5%*
Customer 8	*Down 5%*
Totals	*up/down - percentage and sales*

EXAMPLE: LANDSCAPING RETAILER

COMPONENT	NOTES
Customer 1	*Up $25,000 in purchases -25%*
Customer 2	*Up $15,000 in purchases -15%*
Customer 3	*Up $5,000 in purchases -5%*
Customer 4	*Up $2,000 in purchases -2%*
Customer 5	*down $2,000 in purchases - 2%*
Customer 6	*down $3,000 in purchases - 3%*
Customer 7	*down $10,000 in purchases - 10%*
Customer 8	*down $28,000 in purchases - 28%*
Totals	*total up $47,000, total down $43,000*

PARETO'S PRINCIPLE

I'm sure you've heard of this one. It is also called the 80/20 rule.

But it is much more than just a rule, or even a simple analysis of where the major source of your income comes from.

If you haven't heard of it, here's a quick review of the hypothesis of the model. Basically it says that 80% of your revenue or profit comes from the top 20% of your customers.

The idea is that you should focus your efforts on the best customers who give you the most business, and also be sure you are not investing too much time and money on smaller customers who just aren't right or profitable for you.

The real strategic value of this tool is what you do after this first stage of analysis and action. I've used this tool to remarkable effect on a number of occasions.

In this case a couple of simple case studies is enough explanation in itself. In one case I was leading a small sales team calling on hospitals. With a recent budget cut and layoffs in the team before I took over, the number of people had reduced from 7 to 2 and the budget from $350,000 to $100,000.

The remaining sales team were complaining they didn't have the time to call on all the hospitals with the reduction. They were also worried that budgets remained too high given the company had pulled a lot of investment from this product.

I recognised an opportunity and did an analysis of our top hospital customers. I found the ratio was pretty close to around 20% of the hospitals delivering 80% of our revenue.

I then surveyed those hospitals and found that there was one overriding reason they dealt with us, and it wasn't about the product itself at all. It was because of a novel program we offered as a value add to those hospitals. Detecting infection and cure rates from a variety of products that they used.

The final strategic action was getting the sales team to identify another 20% of the rest of the customers who best matched the size, characteristics and potential of out existing top 20%.

Once they had done that analysis, we stopped all face to face calls on the bottom 60% of customers, and handled them with a call centre.

Then we prioritised calling on the additional 20% we had identified and offered them the value add program, which hadn't previously been available to them. With this, we picked up more valuable customers, reduced the total amount of time necessary for calls by focusing only on high potential ones and we grew the brand by over $1.7m dollars in just one year.

Exceptional and unexpected growth that blew the budget out of the water and won us several awards and acknowledgments. All by using one simple strategic tool and then coming up with some bright ideas to use the information we found.

Whilst the PARETO Principle is sometimes call the 80/20 rule,

these percentages aren't always exactly that. You might have 70% of your revenue come from your top 30%. The more important lesson is that a few customers will drive a lot of your revenue, and that there are often customers in a business who do not contribute any profit, and in fact cost you money to service.

A satisfied customer who buys coffee everyday without complaint could be in your top 20% even in a coffee shop. And that nice customer who buys a coffee once a month, who everyone likes, but holds up your order line talking for half an hour every time they come in may in fact be costing you money. Our advice is to know what customers are profitable for you, and which are not.

ACTIONS ARISING

Strengthen top 20% of customers - adding value to keep

Finding more customers like top 20% - referrals, and other methods to attract(within and external to current bottom 80% list)

CUSTOMERS	NOTES
Top 20% of customers	*% of revenue*
Bottom 80% of customers	*% of revenue*

Methods to divest customers who cost too much to service - selling these customers, deciding not to service etc.

EXAMPLE: FINANCIAL SERVICES COMPANY

CUSTOMERS	NOTES
Top 20% of customers	*35% of revenue*
Bottom 80% of customers	*65% of revenue*

ACTIONS ARISING

1. Introduce referral campaign for top 20% customers - with benefits to them and their referred colleagues.

2. Top 20% customers - christmas gift program

3. Top 20% customers - survey to see what else we can do
4. Assess next 20% and work on growing revenue, increase communication and service
5. Sell bottom 20% of customers to a new broker.
6. Increase prices for the next bottom 20% to either encourage them to live or increase profits on these difficult or costly to service customers

RAPID MARKETING MODEL

Perhaps my proudest achievement in our business has been the creation of a strategic planning model specifically for the marketing department.

This model has supported our overall results in the last twenty years of helping 500 clients achieve more than $2 billion in revenue growth. The R.A.P.I.D Marketing Model has the following 5 steps so named for the letters in the acronym.

Research - understanding markets, customers, competitors and yourself.

Analyse - working out the market opportunities and what will stand in your way, including market trends and data.

Plan - planting a flag in the sand for what you stand for and your market positioning, setting goals, assessing resources

Implement - rolling out your marketing in steps designed to find out what works

Detect - measuring everything and refining your marketing effort over time.

This model is covered in depth in my book - *Get your Marketing Cooking*. It has resulted in us being awarded 6 major marketing awards in addition to the revenue success for our clients.

It has also been expanded into complete marketing systems for major clients, and online marketing resource centres being developed for major corporations including banks, insurance companies and real estate agencies.

I also wanted to share some research we've done with over 2000 small, medium and large business owners in relation to marketing.

This may help you in your business too.

We found that less than 20% of all businesses have a marketing plan. We also found that businesses who do have a marketing plan are quite often far more successful.

We have concluded that having a written marketing plan is one of the keys to having a long lasting and successful business. It is why I included our marketing model here for you.

We also found some other statistics about marketing with these 2000 business owners:

- less than 20% had surveyed their customers in the past 12 months

- less than 5% measured what marketing worked for their business

- the majority of businesses started their marketing at step 4 of our 5 step model - meaning they were missing out on the key strategic insights that come from research, analysis and planning and trying to go straight to implementing a marketing program.

There are a number of conclusions about these statistics, which a successful business will understand. These are:

- if you don't know what customers want, how can you know what to offer them in relation to your products and services

- if you don't know what marketing works, you are inevitably going to be wasting money and time on the marketing that you do implement

- if you haven't decided on a position to take in the market, the market will decide that for you and you might not like the outcome of that.

Marketing - like many other activities in your business - is best handled in a strategic manner - and the strategic model I've provided is a well proven model of marketing.

In fact it has helped us help over 500 clients to more than $2billion in revenue growth.

If you'd like a piece of the growth pie for yourself, then I humbly suggest you consider preparing a proper strategic plan for your business. If you do, I can almost guarantee you will have more success than you are having now.

It might seem painful, but it is well worth the effort and I have personally written over a thousand marketing plans in the past 30 years to add to the proof that being planned is better than operating in the dark and with no information about the consequences of your marketing actions.

In the past twenty years, we've used marketing to:

- Help a major insurance broking firm grow from $100m in revenue to over half a billion

- Contributed to growth of tens of millions in revenue and profit to a steel company's operations

From measuring the results of marketing campaigns. From knowing what to communicate to customers in advertising because we knew what mattered most to them. Marketing planning does not have to be arduous, but invest the time and effort and you will reap the rewards.

OUTLINE OF A STRATEGIC PLAN

Now that we're closing in on the end of this book, I'd like to bring all the previous chapters together and give you a template or outline of the contents of a great strategic plan.

Remember of course, it is your plan, and you don't necessarily need to use all the available strategic tools in your plan.

However, the areas of your plan, should cover the 8 rooms we discussed in previous chapters. I'll place some thoughts on what should be in each of those rooms in terms of plans and resources.

EXECUTIVE SUMMARY

Any good plan that contains a lot of detail will have a short summary of a couple of pages of the highlights of the plan. These highlights might be the revenue and profit projections of your business, key strategic issues you are addressing in the plan, and any other outcomes you are projecting to occur from implementing the plan.

An executive summary is useful to show investors, or perhaps a bank manager or even to share with your team or suppliers. It allows you to quickly give someone an idea of your goals and plans, without going into all the detail of how you will achieve it.

It is also a handy reference for yourself to review regularly and check your progress against the goals.

TRACKING SYSTEM

It is useful to put in your plan a template for your tracking of projects and goals. This could be a one page summary of all key projects with their status, and next actions. This also highlights to anyone reading the plan, that you've worked out how you are going to track progress and milestones and keep control over implementation of the plan.

This tracking template would then be updated weekly or monthly with the actual figures on progress.

STRATEGY ROOM

Of course the strategic plan itself is the key part of the strategy room but you might also mention here the key stakeholders for your plan.

This part of the plan would also contain some key information describing your business, your business model, directors/owners shareholders and a summary of any legal documents you have in place like leases, or contracts with key clients.

Major investments or programs covering the whole of business - like a change of business location would be discussed in this part of your plan. Major new product or service introductions would also be covered here.

Insurances would be covered here.

Tools like the SWOT Analysis fit here.

MARKETING ROOM

This would be a detail of your marketing plan - using the RAPID template provided earlier.

Clearly market information, summaries of client research, competitor analyses and other elements all live here in your plan.

Including a budget of what you are going to spend on marketing and where it will be spent.

Also who is responsible for the marketing - staff or outsourced marketing department and how they are being measured.

This room is also a natural place for the ROI Template - although major programs that you invest in elsewhere in the business can also use this tool.

SALES ROOM

An outline of your sales process, review of top customers, up/down analysis if relevant to show what you are focussing on.

Probably also a review of key sales actions for the year, who is responsible for them and how they will be measured.

Any new business development plans would also be included.

MANAGING MONEY ROOM

The money room section of the plan is your financial plan for the year, any policies you have in place for invoicing, collection, expenses and tax and reserves.

The financial plan should be detailed and include your estimates of revenue and expenses month by month, which can be updated regularly at the end of each month replacing budget numbers with actual numbers.

A good budget allows you to see on one page your progress towards financial objectives.

As well as a budget document, you would probably also include major cashflow analysis, which will show you where in the year you are likely to have issues(if any).

MANAGING QUALITY ROOM

I would include a statement of any quality standards you have set, how they will be handled, and any outstanding issues and actions relating to quality.

Also include how you will handle quality issues during the year and the process of fixing either the item itself or the people making it or delivering it in the case of a service.

CLIENT SERVICE ROOM

This would include first and foremost scheduled or planning product and service development and delivery to clients. If you have major clients who comprise a large percentage of your revenue, you should also detail any specific actions you are going to take with each of these in individual client plans within this room part of the plan.

The client room links with the sales room, so useful to indicate any plans here that are influenced by sales. For instance growing the sales within an existing customer might also fit under the responsibility of your sales team.

MANAGING PEOPLE ROOM

The people room will include a review of your staff, including any key staff or executives and your plans for them. Likewise any key suppliers, partners or stakeholders in your business.

It would also include reference to who is responsible for what and how they are being measured.

Also any major training investments or areas of focus.

If there is growth planned, your recruitment plans would also be included here.

Other documents of note might be a template of your job descriptions and performance review documents and also employment contracts and any legislation relating to people that you are focussing on or covered by.

ADAPT ROOM

Old time sailors had a term they used called the WEATHER EYE. The first known use of the term is 1829 but I suspect the concept goes way back - perhaps even to the first Phoenician Sailors, or maybe even further to those intrepid seafaring peoples that became the settlers of islands throughout the pacific ocean.

This term is a beautiful representation of what you need to be doing in the Adapt Room.

The reason is that keeping an eye on the horizon denotes both some far away and something that will take a while to get to you.

Buying yourself time to adapt to changes in markets is the watchword for a business owner.

In a way this means you can keep surprises to a minimum and have enough time to get ready with your plans and ideas to adapt or pivot. The suddenness of the recent and continuing pandemic left pretty much everyone on the hop. But many market changes do take time, and you will have enough warning if you are keeping a weather eye.

Websters defines this as:

1 : an eye quick to observe coming changes in the weather.
2 : constant and shrewd watchfulness and alertness.

The PESTLE Analysis also naturally fits in this room since it is a review of major trends in your market.

If you've done a really thorough PESTLE Analysis, then you will have identified any specific plans for pivoting your business, introducing new systems, or piloting new products or services or business models and the actions related to all of these should be detailed after the PESTLE Analysis.

BIG LITTLE NOW!

The BIG.Little.Now strategic tool is one I developed as a simple and useful tool to setting and getting goals.

Here's how it works:

Step 1 - fully frame out the big goal that is sought. Write in enough detail to describe what the scene looks like whenthe big goal is achieved.

Step 2 - program out the main little things that need to be done in order to achieve that one big thing over several weeks or months. For example 30/60/90 days.

Step 3 - in each scheduled sprint period - say the next 60 minutes or next day. Pick one little thing and do it NOW

There is a sub-component to this which is the YES.NO tool. This is simply the idea that it is easier to say NO when you have a bigger YES in mind. In other words when you stick to the important stuff. And not get sidelined by someone else's ideas or priorities.

In the diagram you'll see YES and NO included just to remind you of this saying. And to help you keep on track with the items you've identified in Steps 1 to 3 above.

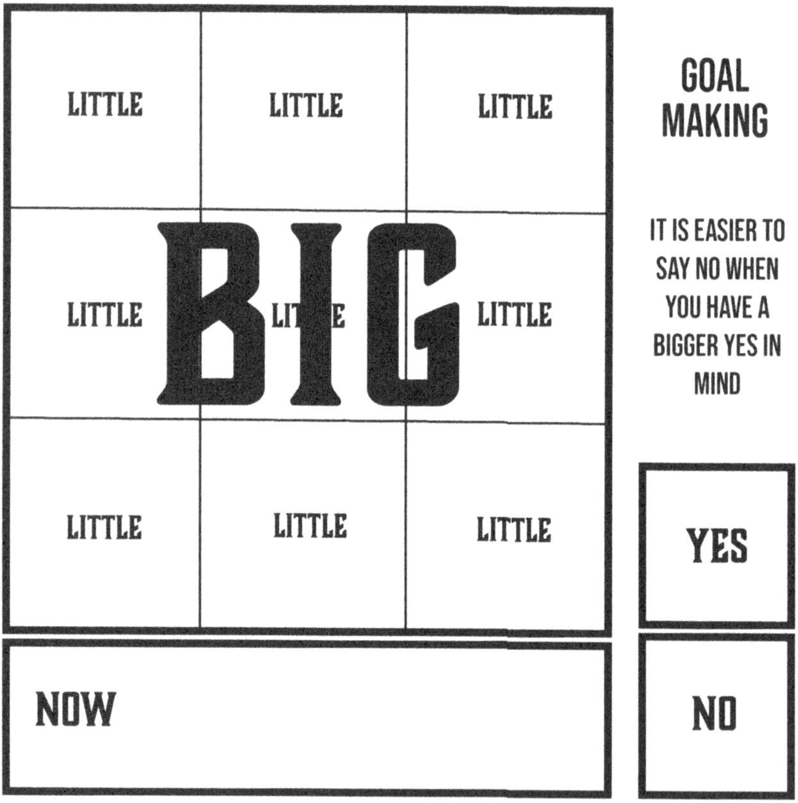

BIG THINGS ARE ACHIEVED BY DOING LITTLE THINGS **NOW!**

CHAPTER FOURTEEN
LEADERSHIP

CHAPTER FOURTEEN- LEADERSHIP

Leadership is an important element of strategy in your business.

I've deliberately left this to last.

All good strategist are leaders, because they want to think ahead into the future, set goals, and then do the things necessary to achieving them.

Leaders, by setting those goals, and putting together plans, actually almost operate in the future. They are thinking ahead, and even doing ahead. They are getting ready for each day the day before.

I wanted to share another article I wrote for the Strategy & Leadership module of our business ownership course, which is also taught to every one of my licensed advisors in my business.

It is also a module in our coaching and we believe the most important module of all for all business owners to understand and execute in their business.

Being a business owner is all about being a leader. Not just to your staff, but also to your customers and to the market as a whole. You need to be planned and organised ahead of your customers.

After all if you didn't think ahead and order those products to put them on the shelf, then they wouldn't be there when your customer is ready to buy them.

Even that simple demonstration of operating in the future should convince you of the importance of being one, two or even several steps ahead of your market, your competition and your customer
.

LEADERSHIP *(reprinted from an article written by the Author in 2018)*

In this article, we're going to give you some tips on being an effective leader. We're also giving you some key tools and resources you can use in leading your team. Don't ever discount the fact that you can lead yourself too. Even in a sole trader situation, by setting goals and being clear, you can inspire yourself to aim high too.

This is by no means an exhaustive list and I'm sure you could find 50 things that people recommend in terms of leadership.
However, being true to our word, we're keeping it simple and concise.

So here goes.

Goals need a why

Whenever you set goals, there has to be a reason for aiming for them.

You need a reason yourself to give you the motivation. There is no point having a goal that no one cares about including yourself. And yet some businesses just blindly set targets for the next year that are effectively a cut and paste from the year before.

Your team needs to be given a reason for achieving a goal. Make it inspiring to them. I guarantee you that they won't be inspired by a 20% growth rate if the only reason for it is to make you rich.

When you set goals, give a reason, and engage your team in the 'what's in it for me' part of it too. Show them how they contribute and how they will win.

Some social and philanthropic goals obviously inspire by their very nature. But in commercial goals, you have to find the personal and group benefit of going for it. Beyond the 'do it or you'll lose your job' style of motivation (not recommended).

An example of a goal and why it could be as simple as this:

We wish to get to $x million in sales this year which represents 10% growth. The reason for this target is we intend expanding our operations into NSW this year, and we need the growth to justify the investment in new offices and staff.

The why is a lot clearer than if you just said – we need to grow by 10%.

BE CLEAR

As a leader it is critically important to be clear when you communicate with your team – clarity in communication ensures people will be able to duplicate what you are trying to do.

Break down goals into understandable components – don't make them hard to understand. Don't be dense in your explanations of plans for your business.

Be clear about the plans, the goals and also what the individuals role is in helping to achieve it. Clarity will increase buy-in.

A great example of a clear goal is that from Elon Musk – we are going to send a manned mission to Mars so we can create an interplanetary civilisation. It's a big goal but it is VERY clear where he is taking the organisation that is SpaceX.

BE CONSISTENT

Some business owners are ALL OVER THE PLACE. They jump from one strategy to the next, one plan to the next and their teams can't keep up with them.

By definition strategies and business goals are usually longer term, so if you're constantly changing the goal posts, how can you expect your team to be able to score?

If you have put enough effort into your strategy, you shouldn't need to change it too often. Sure, conditions change, but these should be the exception rather than the rule. Don't introduce new systems all the time. Don't change your mind every minute.

Be aware of your market, your business and your competition for sure.

But be consistent in your messaging and instructions to your team and you'll be rewarded with a team that knows what it is doing and where it is going.

A classic example of this in the international media at the moment is Donald Trump – he is constantly jumping from one thing to another and it is reported that even his inner circle don't know what is going to happen next. This isn't good leadership, and it certainly doesn't breed confidence and inspiration in his team.

HIRE SMART PEOPLE

An effective leader isn't worried about someone taking their job. They look for SMART people and surround themselves with them. Their calculation is always about whom can I get to do this job brilliantly so I don't have to be concerned with it.

A poor leader is trying to hold onto power or control, and hires ineffective or poorly trained people so they won't ever be made to look bad in their role.

Effective leaders get fast and sustained growth and expansion. Poor leaders do not.

DON'T MICROMANAGE

Leadership has nothing to do with management, and it has even less to do with micro management. Many business owners feel like they are the only ones that can do something right.

And they often insist on others doing it their way. Leaders don't micromanage – EVER!

Today I was introduced to a new piece of software by a new marketing coordinator. This software is so much more effective at handling task-based projects than my existing process, which is to write an action plan and then send it to someone.

If I had insisted that my marketing co-ordinator use my way, then I would never have been open to the new system, which is going to save both them and myself a lot of time and make our work more efficient.

Micro management pisses people off. If they ask for help, help them. But don't hire them and try and do their job for them. What is the point of that?

BE CLEAR ON THEIR ROLE AND YOURS

Everyone loves to know with clarity what their job is. It is amazing how often you hear of people being concerned or upset or confused because they have never been given a clear idea of what their role is. As such, they get a manager who is constantly correcting them, or asking them why such and such hasn't been done.

A business owner who wants to be a strong and effective leader will always be very clear on an employee's role, and also their role as the leader.

With this clarity, everyone can get their job done, not step on someone else's toes, and ensure the big goals are being achieved.

MAKE THEM ACCOUNTABLE/DON'T BE REASONABLE

Being in business is not a halfway house or charity. Yet it is amazing how entitled some employees can be in business today. You may have seen images of companies putting in 'rest pods' to their businesses and all manner of other new age ideas.

A good business owner and leader hires the right people, is clear with what their role is, and makes that person accountable and responsible for achieving the goals and outcomes of that role.

To do otherwise is both pandering and ultimately bad for the business AND the employee.

People like to know what their job is, and they like to be rewarded and recognised for being effective in that role.

If you don't make them responsible and accountable you can almost guarantee they won't perform and if goals aren't met, they'll blame you or someone else.

This does not mean being a tyrant or abusing staff.

But definitely hold them accountable to do their job, provide them with the resources to do it, support them. But don't pander or be reasonable if they don't get it done.

BE FAIR, BE HUMAN AND STAY TRUE

There are many legislative protections for employees these days. All have come about from abuses of the basic rights or from lack of responsibility and humanity from business owners.

Without getting into a wide range of specifics there are three things you must do as a leader and business owner.

Be fair to the person, treat them as a human, and stay true to them, yourself and the business. In your heart, you know what the right way is to treat people. You don't need legislation to tell you that.

By being fair, human and true you will inspire individuals to follow you not just because they have a target, but because they respect you and want to help you get your goals.

They will follow you for who you are, not just because you pay them.

ABOUT THE AUTHOR

Hunter Leonard has always been a goal-maker. From a young age he was upsetting his mother for bringing a broad range of insects, spiders and amphibians into the house, and then letting many of them roam around his bedroom unattended.

As a young boy he often set targets for himself in sport and play - and then persistently practising and putting in the effort to reach them.

In his corporate career, in pharmaceuticals and then Healthcare Advertising, Hunter developed a reputation for innovative and leading edge thinking. He always listened to customers and researched ideas before coming up with programs and innovations that turned markets on their heads.

He created a concept for a cross functional project team that became an international model for product launches; a new business program that helped his agency win 12 of 13 pitches in one year. Even as a young sales representative he saw market opportunities in hospitals that resulted in his company securing almost un-winnable business against generic products. He rapidly increased sales of products in his marketing care with novel target marketing programs.

This pattern has continued with the creation of multiple alternative marketing models for clients that have delivered returns on investment unheard of in marketing. Some up to seventy times the investment in the program.

As a business owner, Hunter has run a well-respected advisory business for over twenty years, using smart market insights, deep thinking and designed processes to help over 500 clients achieve more than $2billion in revenue growth.

Hunter is the author of ten books - including this one - hundreds of articles, dozens of poems, a few short science fiction stories and even some songs. In total he calculates he has written over 8 million words in one form or another over the last two decades.

He has delivered over 750 presentations, seminars, keynotes and workshops. He has surveyed well over ten thousand business owners, whilst conducting surveys with hundreds of thousands of responses for clients.

Hunter is also a passionate advocate for human rights and in particular Article #23 of the UN Declaration of Human Rights - The Right to Work.

His interests include cooking, photography, music and the beautiful Australian Bushland.

For Hunter, there is nothing better than setting and achieving a worthwhile goal.

And he definitely likes coloured animals.

You can read more of Hunter's work and connect with him on Linkedin - ***https://www.linkedin.com/in/hunter-leonard/***

ABOUT RED-G

Red-G is a fairly typical adolescent male giraffe.

In the absence of a biography, here are 11 fun facts about giraffes like Red G.

Of course, not many giraffes can do a strategy like Red-G, but he is one very talented giraffe.

1. Giraffes are the tallest mammals on Earth. Their legs alone are taller than many humans—about 6 feet.[1]

2. They can run as fast as 35 miles an hour over short disances, or cruise at 10 mph over longer distances.[2]

3. A giraffe's neck is too short to reach the ground. As a result, it has to awkwardly spread its front legs or kneel to reach the ground for a drink of water.[3]

4. Giraffes only need to drink once every few days. Most of their water comes from all the plants they eat.[4]

5. Giraffes spend most of their lives standing up; they even sleep and give birth standing up.[5]

6. The giraffe calf can stand up and walk after about an hour and within a week, it starts to sample vegetation.[6]

7. Despite the females' attempts to stand over their calves during attacks by lions, spotted hyenas, leopards and African wild dogs (4), many calves are killed in their first few months[7]

8. A giraffe's spots are much like human fingerprints. No two individual giraffes have exactly the same pattern.[8]

9. Both male and female giraffes have two distinct, hair-covered horns called ossicones. Male giraffes use their horns to sometimes fight with other males.[9]

10. Giraffes only need 5 to 30 minutes of sleep in a 24-hour period! They often achieve that in quick naps that may last only a minute or two at a time.[10]

11. Whilst it was thought that giraffes did not make any sounds, this is now known to be untrue, as giraffes bellow, snort, hiss and make flute-like sounds, as well as low pitch noises beyond the range of human hearings [11]

ABOUT BLUE FROG MARKETING

Blue Frog is an independent, privately-owned strategic advisory business servicing clients in Australia and overseas, since 2001. It is owned and run by the co-founders and directors - Nicole and Hunter Leonard. They are supported by a large network of skilled professionals including digital marketers, printers, videographers and many more.

Blue Frog has generated a remarkable reputation with business owners - small and large - for providing workable strategic advice. And stunning results, delivering over $2 billion in revenue growth for over 500 clients since 2001.

The philosophy at Blue Frog is that market success will only come from a deep understanding of the market, the customer, the competition and yourself. And that turning these insights into brilliant strategic plans will deliver the results with far more prediction that operating in an ad-hoc, unplanned manner.

With proprietary market models, and a willingness to go where no one has gone before in developing innovative market-leading programs, Blue Frog has delivered some phenomenally successful programs for clients over the last twenty years and garnered quite a few acknowledgements along the way.

With experience working in markets from industrial to retail, financial services to healthcare, real estate to crop protection, recycling to health food, there are few markets or segments that Blue Frog has not touched.

The team are also known for their care, respect and blisteringly fast service that other simply can't compete with.

Whilst they fly under the radar compared to other higher profile strategic groups, there is no doubt that partnering with Blue Frog has delivered significant returns on investment for many clients.

To find out what Blue Frog can do for your organisation, book in a discussion.

One service that clients rave about is our half day Red Giraffe session where you get to nominate your goals and then work with our team to map out exactly what it will take to reach them.

In a half day Red Giraffe Session we'll build a strong framework for your strategic planning and populate it with key actions that will set you on the road to success.

Key actions we'll take include:

1. Assessing your goals and putting them under the reality microscope
2. Looking at your current situation
3. Listing out the top strategic actions that will take you from here to there
4.Fill up your strategic toolkit with a range of tools discussed in this book and populated with the best available knowledge from your team and ours
5. Identify gaps and risks, strengths and opportunities
6. Map out a pathway to success with agreed timelines

For a relatively small investment, this session could save you hundreds of thousands in time, energy and money. It already has for dozens of our clients in the past ten years.

Just reach out to us at ***hunter@bluefrogmarketing.com.au*** or call 0400237647.

ABOUT CONSIGLI8

Consigli8 was founded in 2021 as a joint venture between Silver & Wise and Finwell Group. It uses all the content and intellectual property and is based on surveys of over ten thousand business owners.

In this advisory business our advisors deliver our 8 Rooms Method as discussed in this book.

Our services include bespoke advisory and educational content in the form of courses and resources across all 8 rooms.

Your journey with Consigli8 starts with our proprietary Diagnostic Service where we benchmark your current situation in all 8 Rooms and then build a detailed action plan across those 8 rooms to help you grow your business or set it up to support the lifestyle you want.

You can find out more at ***www.consigli8.com***

THE ARTICLE THAT STARTED IT ALL

Back in 2014, the very first article I wrote on Linkedin - of a total of 136 articles on that platform - was about business owners becoming generalists instead of specialists.

At the time I was working on a concept that would eventually become our strategic consulting service for business owners.

I'm reprinting this article as an addendum to this book on strategy as a little bit of history as to how long I've been thinking about how we can help more business owners become more strategic.

SMALL BUSINESS OWNERS - SPECIALISTS WHO NEED TO GENERALISE

by Hunter Leonard, first published Sept 19th, 2014.

I've found an interesting dynamic in the last 15 years of running my own SME. In benchmarking the marketing practices of over 1000 small businesses, I found something very compelling in the behaviour of these business owners - they are almost all specialists in their field, but equally very few are generalists.

Most got into their business because they were technical experts in a chosen field - maybe they had worked at this occupation in a larger organisation. And they had a passion to do it for themselves.

Unfortunately, they then go and start a business and run into the biggest barrier to their success in the future - being able to generalise.

In bigger business, the corporate world if you like, you have a wide range of specialists all doing their specific task - the HR, finance, marketing, sales, production, quality control etc etc.

In running a small business, many people realise they have to do it all, there isn't an expert in 'x' down the hall they can call on. Sure they can outsource, but eventually all business owners run into the issue that they just aren't trained to be a business owner.

I'm working on a project at the moment which is designed to help business owners - small and large - become a generalist. And I don't mean knowing a little about a lot of things.

I firmly believe that the SME segment of our economy, the backbone of our economy, needs business owners to step up and become better generalists. They need to know how to plan strategy for their business, they need to know how to handle HR/People issues, they need to know what product or service their business is in the business of producing, and how to get it produced at high quality. They need to know how to generate referrals and word of mouth.

Because, like the specialist species who can only eat one food type, or can only survive in one environment - time is short for the business owner who is a technical specialist in their field, but doesn't know how to handle money, or people or marketing.

Here's to a future of business owners being better generalists.

ARE YOU ON PURPOSE?

I originally wrote this article for SMALLVILLE - a portal featuring some wonderful writers and consultants sharing their tips for small business owners. The SMALLVILLE Community was created by the big daddy of all business authors in Australia - Andrew Griffiths.

Andrew is an entrepreneurial futurist with a deep passion for helping business owners be their best.

Here's the article.

ARE YOU ON PURPOSE? *(originally published June 2018)*

The culture and history of Japan fills me with awe, admiration and enjoyment. For many years, I've collected rare tin robots from the golden age of Science Fiction and the best of these come from Osaka in Japan. The logo of our marketing business for many years was an origami frog, and when searching for a philosophical foundation for our new business – Silver and Wise – I found and selected the Japanese philosophy of IKI-GAI – which is considered to be Japan's secret to a long and healthy life.

As our passion is to help mature entrepreneurs start their first business in their 40's and beyond and eastern cultures appear to be far more reverent of experience and wisdom than western ones, I find this philosophy also applicable in the search for an decision on what sort of business you should run.

In this article, I examine the four intertwined concepts of IKI-GAI (pronounced Ick-ee-guy) and how you can apply them to this choice.

In this diagram of IKI-GAI you see four intersecting circles – what you love, what the world needs, what you are good at, and finally what you can be paid for. At the intersection of each pair we have mission, vocation, profession and passion and at the centre of all these is the nexus or IKI-GAI – loosely meaning "your reason for being" or as I have translated – Purpose.

And so I ask you four questions – the answers of which will help you decide on a business opportunity for yourself.

What do you love? – running a business you'll have good days and bad days – but if you love what you are doing, you'll be able to push through challenges to the other side without feeling like you should be doing something else. If there is no inner passion for what you do, it will be all about the money and this isn't good for you, your staff or your customers. In small business it's the human element that gives us an advantage over the big competitors – and if there is no heart in our business people will notice

What does the world need? – I know it may seem like all our needs and wants are catered for in the world today. But if you examine every market closely, and at the local level you intend on operating, I will make you a bet you can find a market opening or niche that needs filling.

It may be a faster delivered dry cleaned suit, it may be an organic café, it may be a plumber who doesn't leave a mess and turns up on time. Accurately researching your chosen market and your ideal customer will open up opportunities which you can take advantage of.

The trouble is, in our surveys of business owners, too few are surveying their market and customer enough to really know these needs well.

What can you be paid for? – I'm sure we all know inherently that to be paid for something we have to deliver value.

But working in a job sometimes there is a disconnect between our pay and what we do on a daily basis. In business, you soon find out if your customers value your product or service highly enough – because you'll start making money and profit. If they don't you won't – it's pretty simple – so can you get paid enough for what you are going to do to make a profit and an income. I suggest you find this out in your research too.

What are you good at? – many people who start a business have a deep technical skills in something related to the products or services of their business idea.

This is good, but if you remain a technical expert at delivering products and services, you'll get stuck in the day to day grind of your business. In order to be a successful business owner there are 8 skills and systems you need to put in place.

Better to be skilled at being a business owner, than making violins if that is your business. Business Owners can get others to make and deliver product, whilst they focus on scaling their business and working on it. So make sure you're a good business owner if you decide to start a business.

Japan is a wondrous and history filled culture. The philosophy of Iki-gai is a simple intersection of four elements which I believe can contribute to a highly successful life in business if you examine, research and apply them to your right business choice and make sure you know each factor well in relation to that business choice.

Of course, what I've presented here is a westernised concept of Ikigai and doesn't necessarily reflect all that this word and concept implies within the Japanese culture.

Best wishes for starting your new business. Reach out and tell me how you go.

HOW TO SET AND REACH YOUR GOALS

The twin skills of strategy and leadership.

This is another short article that featured on SMALLVILLE in March 2018. This article was another useful in the genesis of this book and making strategy more approachable for business owners.

Want to know the difference between a wish and a goal?

The former is a wishy washy hope that something good might happen in your future. The latter is something you back with action to make sure it occurs.

In this article, I want to discuss with you the twin skills of strategy and leadership are the key to helping you set and achieve goals in your business.

The key word however is ACTION – you have to DO something to be the kind of person who can set and reach goals.

Firstly, a goal really has to be real for you to have any chance of reaching it. You should absolutely dream big, but goals need to be specific, measurable, achievable, realistic and time bound – in other words S.M.A.R.T.

To set smart goals you do need a measure of competence in understanding the environment you operate in, and what it is possible to achieve with the customers you want to target, the resources you have at your disposal and the competitors you face.

This takes a program of research and developing an understanding of these dynamics, which is all part of the first skill – STRATEGY. This is one of those words in business which is thrown about with abandon, but you may be surprised to know it actually does mean something very specific.

I'm not going to use a dictionary definition here, but rather explain the concept. Effectively STRATEGY means a set of tools and actions designed to help a person or business achieve the goals they have set for themselves – usually over the longer term. It is HOW you are going to achieve your goals.

This toolkit we've defined includes things such as:

- A market research program
- SWOT Analysis
- PESTLE Analysis
- Competitor Analysis
- Value Proposition
- Business Model
- Pricing

This is just for starters.

So you can see it isn't some mysterious term – but rather a set of actions to achieve a goal.

Our second skill in the microscope for today's article is LEADERSHIP.

This is the WHY of getting to a goal.

No matter if we are a sole trader or the owner of a large corporation, the one constant in business is we are surrounded by other people who we have to influence to get to our goals.

Whether this be customers, or stakeholders, or our board, or investors – whoever.

As the founder and owner of your business, you are by definition a leader. But to become an effective and successful leader, you have to be able to influence people to follow you on your journey. Or to support you on your journey – for instance – getting a bank manager to loan you money.

This requires you to be able to clearly define the goals you've set and to convince them you can achieve these goals, and that joining you on this journey would be valuable, remunerative or enjoyable for them.

A leader should be able to:

- Communicate goals
- Let people know what their role is on the journey
- Keep people informed as you progress

- Reward those who help you achieve the goals, and get those who are stopping or hindering you out of the way

So there you go – set and achieve your goals with the twin skills of strategy and leadership. Learn, understand and use the tools available to make your dreams a reality.

APPENDICES

PARTICIPATE IN A GOAL SETTERS/GOAL GETTERS CHALLENGE OR GROUP PROGRAM

Have you ever wanted to get really great at achieving your goals?

Most people have wished for this at one stage or another.

Would you like to learn from someone who has led a team that has achieved this for over 500 clients - generating more than $2billion in revenue growth as a result?

What would that be worth to you?

There is a method you can use to set and get your goals.

For the first time ever, I'm going to mentor a small tribe of business owners on a couple of very special journeys.

PROGRAM 1 - THE 21 DAY GOAL SETTERS/GOAL GETTERS CHALLENGE

Over 21 days, you'll join up to 100 others in the ultimate goal setting and goal getting challenge. Learn new skills, meet other business owners, build a community, have fun and win prizes.

To find out more about our next 21 Day
Goal Getters/Goal Setters challenge, email the author at
hunter@bluefrogmarketing.com.au

PROGRAM 2 - THE 7- MONTH GOAL SETTERS/GOAL GETTERS JOURNEY

Over the course of seven months, you'll join with a small exclusive group of participants in this program that will change your life when it comes to setting and getting your goals.

Each month, there will be a group strategy session, you'll get books, courses, resources and a monthly campfire session to share progress with your fellow participants.

What we'll cover:

Month 1 - The Undiscovered Country - sitting there at your desk you can perceive the world around you. The sights, smells, sounds of your office or some other location you enjoy. But the future is the Undiscovered Country - as named by Shakespeare in Hamlets 'to be or not to be' soliloquy.

So how do you make the future more real to you? How do you plant a goal firmly in the future and then craft it and describe it so it becomes an inspiring 'guidon' to reach for? How do you turn a mere wish into an achievable goal?

Month 2 - The Honest Now

A key ingredient after you've set a goal is to honestly assess the now. We then call this month - The Honest Now. What do you need to define, describe and identify in your current situation.

Why is this the other anchor point in any true goal setting, goal getting program?

Month 3 - What's the difference.

Once you've described your desired future, and your honest now, what is there left to do? You can just sit back and relax right? No! What we'll cover this month is the skill of playing spot the difference. Right now as you get ready to start your journey to achieving your goals, this skill of spotting the difference will be a valuable tool all the way to your destination.

Month 4 - Bright Ideas

Ok, this month we'll talk about strategy and bright ideas. The human condition of aiming for desirable ends with available means. We'll review your strategic tool kit, practice with each of these tools at length. And get ready for the next step on the journey.

Month 5 - Leg Work

This is literally where the rubber hits the road in getting to your goals. Leg work sounds like it might be hard. But nothing could be further from the truth. Actually, it is more about alignment and persistence on a given course. Our program shows how you make the impossible possible and the hard easy. With the right tools in place and a commitment to do the work in increments, you can achieve any goal.

Month 6 - The journey (and the dreaded shiny object tree)

Once you are on the journey and using all the tools you have available to you, things will get easier. But wait, what about bright shiny objects? This month we will talk about the journey, the milestones in particular and how to avoid bright shiny objects.

This is a critical phase in our program and one that you will really enjoy.

Especially when you find out the solution to why most people don't get to their goals.

Month 7 - The transit lounge -

Ok you get off that long flight, stretch your legs and enjoy the feeling of having arrived at your destination. Time for a celebration.

Yes and No.

We'll definitely celebrate this month for sure. It signals the completion of the program and your graduation as a Goal Setter/ Goal getter - and there will be prizes and acknowledgements. But we will also chat about why your arrival should actually be treated more like a transit lounge.

Why? Well you'll find out in this final month of the program.

Sound like you?

There are two ways you can participate in this program.

"Camping Model" - you can join us on the journey as a group participant, get the book, course, resources, and a monthly group webinar. As well as a mid-month campfire session with your fellow program participants where you can share your progress on the journey.

There are only 24 places available in each Camping Journey. Within this total, you will be assigned to your own walking group of up to 6 companions. Your team will participate as a team throughout the program and attend your own monthly campfire sessions. You'll also help and hold accountable this small group to completing the journey together.

"Glamping Model"- you'll get all of the above, but with some extra special 1000 thread count service along the way. The Glamping Journey includes a fortnightly 1-2-1 session(14 sessions in total) with our head ranger. In this session, we'll dissect the content on a deeper more personal level for you and your business. You can raise any specific items you want to cover and get personal help on your goal setting and getting. Due to time constraints on the journey, this option is only available to 6 participants who select it within each 7-month program. You can find out more by emailing the author at ***hunter@bluefrogmarketing.com.au.***

WANT TO EMBRACE BEING A LITTLE MORE STRATEGIC?

If something in this book piqued your interest, or you need help, why not reach out and have a chat with Hunter.

We have a number of strategic services and mentoring programs for organisations and individuals that could be deployed to assist you.

Check out the following pages, our website www.bluefrogmarketing.com.au or reach out direct at hunter@bluefrogmarketing.com.au.

STRATEGIC WORKSHOP

It might seem impossible, but in a few short hours, our team can help you extract the framework for your business strategy and get it into a detailed action planning document ready for you to implement.

Before the workshop, you'll receive a brief on what information to prepare. On the day, we'll work with you and your key people to decipher this information and build your strategic framework.

"I came across Hunter for the first time when i happened to reply to one of his posts on Linked In. He interpreted my vision well and was able to capture it within a strategic plan which straightened our focus and effort." (Client, Australia)

Book a conversation by email hunter@bluefrogmarketing.com.au

NEED A SPEAKER OR MC?

Hunter believes in evidence-based solutions and has surveyed more than 10,000 business owners to develop the services offered by his organisations. He has delivered over 750 keynotes, seminars and presentations and contributed to over $2 billion in sales growth for his 500+ clients since 2001.

He is highly regarded for his warmth, generosity, innovative thinking and his ability to get measurable results for his clients. Hunter is available for either MC duties or to deliver keynotes on topics such as ageism, mature age work, the future of work, strategy and marketing.

Speaker Kit, Showreel and Rates available on request by calling emailing hunter@bluefrogmarketing.com.au

COACH OR MENTOR?

The team at Blue Frog Marketing have coached and mentored thousands of current and aspiring business owners. We have a range of coaching services ranging from basic introductory 1-2-1 sessions on business readiness through to ongoing coaching and mentoring of business owners.

"I have had the pleasure of working with Hunter on a number of events designed to support mature age business owners in Australia. Hunter is not only a pioneer, having surveyed over 10,000 mature aged business owners, but a passionate marketing expert making his material engaging, relatable and not to be missed. Hunters a seasoned professional when it comes to his speaking engagements, clearly delivering his message whilst supporting the causes near and dear to his heart." Natalie Brookes

Book in a confidential discussion -
hunter@bluefrogmarketing.com.au

WANT MORE BOOKS?

When not running his business, Hunter is also the best selling author of ten books including this one - **Red Giraffe** and a Science Fiction Novella - Genetech P.S. He has also - by the way - written hundreds of articles, dozens of songs and poems and several short children's stories. He is also an accomplished ghost writer writing several books for clients including business books and family histories.

A percentage of the profits from book sales are donated to charitable organisations working to improve human rights or reduce human rights abuses. Whether you want to buy books for yourself or your team signed by the author you can order at online at bluefrogmarketing.com.au.

We offer discounted rates for bulk purchases.

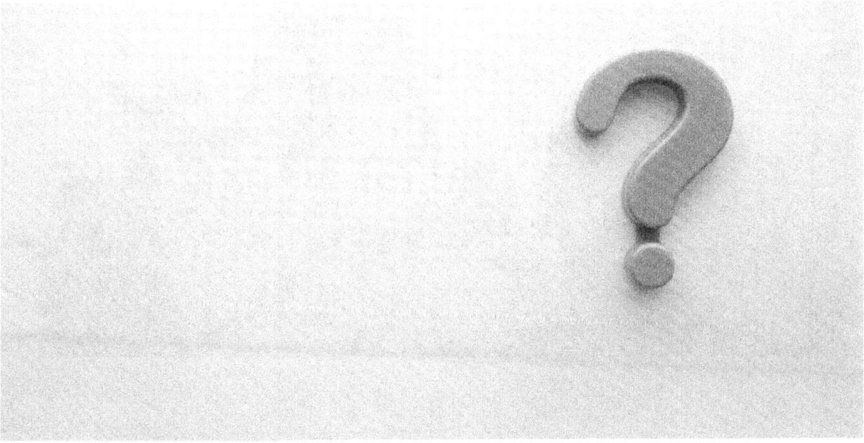

SOMETHING ELSE?

Whether you are in a government department, not for profit organisation or a corporate, we can help you with bespoke programs that match your needs.

No one knows more about the needs of organisations when it comes to strategic planning.

We literally wrote the book on it.

But seriously, we are more than happy to chat with you to understand your specific needs and then adapt our existing intellectual property, programs or co-create something just for you.

If it helps with our vision of a world where more organisations are setting and getting their goals, we'd be honoured and delighted to help you.

Email us at hunter@bluefrogmarketing.com.au

INTERVIEWS AND ARTICLES?

Hunter is an accomplished writer and interviewer or interviewee.

If you need articles for your publication on anything to do with mature age work, strategy, marketing or business ownership, Hunter would be delighted to write for you.

He has featured in national and international media and on podcasts all over the world. Interviews on ABC radio, Channel 7, Sky News, Virgin Magazine, In the Black, Sydney Morning Herald. Guest appearances on The Blank Canvas, DENT Global Podcast, Kickass Boomers, Inspire Business for Good and many more.

For a confidential discussion or to book an interview please email us at hunter@bluefrogmarketing.com.au